Blessings on you

Mary Anna
and
Charles H. Grant —

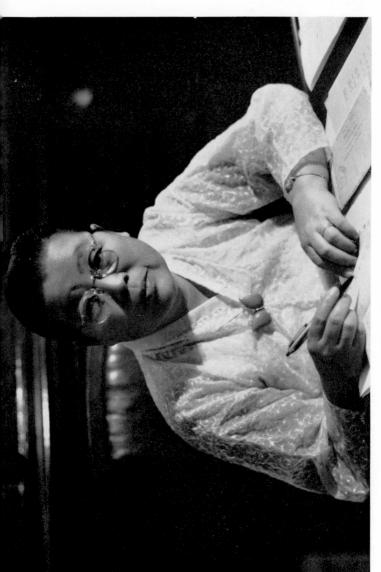

DR. HELEN KIM

GRACE SUFFICIENT

The Story of Helen Kim

by

Herself

Edited by J. Manning Potts

The Upper Room
The World's Most Widely Used Devotional Guide
and
OTHER DEVOTIONAL LITERATURE
1908 Grand Avenue
Nashville, Tennessee 37203

Library of Congress Catalog Card Number: 64-24071

UR-198-15-0964
Printed in the United States of America

In my lifelong experience of God's grace I have always found it to be just enough—in other words, sufficient. God has never been extravagant, or stingy, in His constant bestowal of grace.
—Helen Kim

INTRODUCTION

It has been my privilege to write introductions to several books, but none has given me more pleasure than this one in tribute to Helen Kim.

No woman I have known has achieved so much, or influenced so many lives, or done so much to elevate the status of women. No woman has been involved in more international organizations. The world has built a pathway to her door at Ewha Womans University.

Helen Kim had a great mother who was a first generation Christian and who brought her whole family into the Christian Church. Prayer was a significant part of her family life and has always been a significant part of Helen's life.

When Helen was sixteen she herself had a great experience of Christ after a night of vigil and prayer. Mrs. Thomas Nicholson, the widow of Bishop Nicholson and for many years president of the Woman's Foreign Missionary Society of the Methodist Episcopal Church, wrote of the influence of this spiritual awakening on the life of Helen Kim:

> Her purpose became more constructive and definite. It had been political—to help free her country from alien power. Hereafter she would spend her life in helping to free her countrywomen from the traditions and prejudices that limited their contribution to life. She took Korean women from behind the curtain of nonentity and set them in the midst of the life of their people, trained to help their country solve its problems.

In time Helen graduated from Ewha College, from Ohio Wesleyan University with a BA degree, from Boston University Graduate School with an MA, and from Teachers College of Columbia University with a

PhD. Phi Beta Kappa membership, honorary degrees, citations for meritorious service were bestowed on her. From a scholarship pupil in the little Ewha Haktang—first school for girls in Korea—she rose to the presidency of Ewha Womans University, the largest university for women in the world.

What has been the driving force of this diminutive woman less than five feet in height, whose tiny foot fits into a size three shoe? There is only one answer. She has been dominated by her faith in Christ. Without faith there is no explanation of Helen Kim.

It has been a great privilege to work with Helen in editing this book. We talked about the title, GRACE SUFFICIENT, and Helen explained: "The title came to me as a summary of my life." So this is the story of GRACE SUFFICIENT as revealed in the life of Helen Kim. It is a great story of a great woman. It is also an interesting history of political movements in Korea in her lifetime.

It has been a privilege to be assisted by Mrs. Paul McKnight as we have worked on the editing of the book. She has done more than I have. Mrs. Robert Ashford, who has done the typing, has shown great interest in the manuscript. We pray that the book will make Helen Kim better known and that her witness for Christ may have an even wider range in the world. We pray also that it will awaken more prayers and concern for that remarkable institution, Ewha Womans University.

J. MANNING POTTS
Editor, *The Upper Room*
Nashville, Tennessee

CONTENTS

CONTENTS

PREFACE

Several friends insisted during recent years that I write the story of my life. However, this is so contrary to my upbringing in Korean etiquette as well as to my natural shyness, that my answer was always no, usually with the excuse that I had no time. They would always come back at me saying, "But only you can write it, for no other person is in the position to do it. You have gone through so much of your life alone."

Inadvertently, my retirement came earlier than expected and I lost my covenient alibi. And so I yielded to the insistence of my friends.

Friends persuaded me to write my story, and I have written it for them. They did not convince me that it is worth going on record, but they fully assured me of their desire for it. Each of you also who reads this story is my friend. I am taking you into full confidence, as a friend who chats with friends.

The logical principle that would follow such a setting is truthfulness as absolute as humanly possible. Only actual experiences of visible or invisible nature have been recorded. No decorations and no fancies have been allowed, even if their use might have improved the story in style or substance. I have not found it necessary or wise to tell everything, but whatever is written is true.

A second principle I have followed is objectivity. You may ask, is that possible? Yes, it is, again under human limitations. After all, objectivity is a state of mind. Any person with a normal psychology can command it at will and it is possible to maintain objectivity in dealing with one's own story.

ix

I wish to express my appreciation to Miss Marion Conrow, a lifelong friend, and to Miss Frances Fulton for their assistance in the original drafting of this manuscript. I wish to acknowledge also the stimulating help of Mr. Harold Isaacs in the first stages of writing it; and I am grateful to Miss Mildren Owen, another lifelong friend, who contributed so many helpful suggestions in the rewriting of the manuscript. I owe a great debt to my secretaries, Mrs. Yun-sook Yoo Lee and Mrs. Young-sook Chu Lee, for their tireless work in copying and recopying the manuscript. Without all this help and assistance the work could not have been completed.

—HELEN KIM

I

ARRIVAL IN A HAPPY HOME

Chemulpo was a very important port city to which my father, Mr. Chin Yawn Kim, moved from Eui-ju in the northwestern part of Korea. This city is more commonly known as Inchon. A large statue of General Douglas MacArthur stands on top of a hill overlooking the bay in commemoration of the amphibious landing of September, 1950.

Chemulpo, or Inchon, in the late nineteenth century was a newly booming seaport town about twenty-five miles from the capital city of Seoul. Korea for centuries had been a hermit nation, for her encounters with other nations had always been unfortunate. With China, Russia, and Japan, Korea's international relations were always difficult and almost forced the kings to keep the gates tightly closed. But this was no longer possible, and Korea had recently abandoned her traditional policy of isolation and opened her doors to other nations. Ships were coming in from the West as well as from Japan. At Chemulpo the first treaty of amity and commerce with a Western country, the United States of America, was signed in 1882.

The importance of this seaport was felt throughout the country. Adventurous spirits were gathering in from all parts of the nation. One of these men was my father. He had inherited a good-size farm from his father, but not the traits of a good farmer. He was more of a scholar according to the Confucian school. So after settling on the farm his nephew, whom he had reared after his brother's death, and his own son by

1

his first wife, my father had migrated down to Chemulpo late in 1870 in search of new opportunity and better living.

He entered into the wholesale business and met with a reasonable measure of success. He had become a widower a few years before coming to Chemulpo, and now felt he could afford a new wife. Several friends and middlemen introduced to him many candidates for marriage, but he decided on mother, who had also come from Eui-ju. A modest wedding took place and a new home was founded. Sons and daughters kept coming to them. When I arrived there were already four sisters and two brothers. After me came another brother; so we were eight altogether.

When they were expecting my birth everybody in the family, as well as neighbors and friends, wanted a boy. There were too many girls already, they felt, and a fifth daughter would be a bad omen. But mother was more or less prepared. She said she had a dream at the time of conception in which she saw what seemed to be a tiger jumping down into her yard from the roof, indicating that it was being sent from above. She was very happy and looked at it more closely, only to find that it was a dog and not a tiger. But she loved the dog just the same and treasured it as a gift from heaven. She interpreted her dream to mean that her new baby was to be a daughter. According to the way of thinking at that time, a tiger would represent a male with strength and importance; but the dog, which was considered to be of much less value, would mean only a female. Such discriminatory ideas about the two sexes were rampant in those days.

On February 27, 1899, I was born into this happy family of Kims, humble in station, poor in material possessions, but rich in family devotion and loyalty. Although at first I was not very welcome, very soon I was loved and cherished by all the members of the family.

According to family practice in naming the daughters, I was called Kideuk which means "gained in the year of *Ki-hai*." In Korea we name the years, months, days, and hours by a cycle of twelve animals. They are pig, rat, ox, tiger, rabbit, dragon, serpent, horse, sheep, monkey, rooster, and dog. The year 1899 was called *Ki-hai*, the pig's year. So my name merely meant "obtained in the pig's year."

My family did better than others, for in many cases girls were not important enough to be given a name at all. They were known as daughters of their fathers in childhood, wives of their husbands and mothers of their sons throughout life. They did not need any names of their own. In contrast, when boys were born families spent time and money going to professional namers who resorted to all their knowledge of zodiacal signs and the mysterious combinations of the *eum* and *yang*, negative and positive forces in all creation. It was so important to find and give a good name to a boy because it was believed that much of his future would be determined by his name.

Although father was doing well in his business, the size of his family was outgrowing his purse. By the time I arrived mother had initiated several projects to supplement the family budget. For instance, she raised hogs and chickens, and she made a great deal of extra soy sauce to sell. She was always busy and had to be away from home a great deal. I often missed my mother's milk and grew up on rice gruel. My third sister Ellen, eight years older than I, had the responsibility of taking

3

care of me in mother's absence. Sister Ellen told me later in life that whenever she fed me the rice gruel, I became so contented that I went right back to sleep. Mischievous brothers used to look down on me and teased, "She surely is a pig. She eats and sleeps all the time!" But this endeared me to sister all the more. I became a pleasant responsibility for her. When she wanted to go out and play with other children or climb the hills nearby, she took me on her back. I usually slept the whole time.

Our spacious thatched-roof house and large walled courtyard stood at the edge of the town without any neighboring houses close by. Just outside the gate lay the wide fields for vegetables and grains. A shallow stream ran by the front of the house, and hills and mountains stood beyond in the distance. Sister Ellen used to wade in the stream and climb the mountains with me on her back. She said the only time she felt her burden really heavy was the time she tried to take hold of the clouds in the sky. Standing at the foot of the nearest hill, she saw the sky resting on its top. When she got to the top she saw it on top of the next hill. She wanted so much to reach the sky, so she scaled the hills one after another to catch and feel the clouds. She returned home that night tired and hungry and keenly disappointed. I must have shared her intense feeling, for from this time on a special bond of affection and devotion grew between us. Among the eight of us I was always her favorite and she was mine.

Our family washdays were like picnics. After breakfast the women members of the household were out by the stream where we sat down and washed the clothes, beating out the dirt against small flat stones with smoothly cut sticks. We boiled the very soiled clothes over a temporary fireplace. I could not do any heavy work but was always happy to run around and look after the clothes laid out on sunny spots to dry. When the wind blew, even mildly, I had to jump here and there to hold them down. At lunch time we sat in a circle by the stream and enjoyed the food as though we were starving. To this day womenfolk gather like this at a stream or a river and carry on social life, visiting and gossiping along with their washing.

Korean houses are built around a court or open space in the form of a square in which are planted flowers and small trees. The floors of the living and sleeping rooms are made of stone and mud and covered with thick oiled paper. Under these rooms are long flues which carry the heat from a small stone furnace set into the floor.

Our living rooms were *an-bang* and *maru,* the biggest with heated floor for winter and the other with unheated wooden floor for summer. These two rooms were used by mother and the smaller children, and all the major events within the family took place here. Across the *maru* were smaller rooms for my grown-up sisters and their friends. This part of the house was called the women's quarters. My father, his sons, and their guests occupied another group of rooms built around a second court.

The happy and carefree days of my early childhood were all one could wish for. When too many playmates assembled and got in mother's way, she used to tell us to go outside to play. The big courtyard within the outer wall was our playground. There was a favorite spot on the southeast side, sunny and quiet. We set up a playhouse against the wall and made a small doll family. Large and small stones, odd-size pieces of wood and cardboard, and mud were used as materials to build the

5

house and furnish the interior decorations. Broken pieces of chinaware and bits of wood and twigs were used on the table as dishes and chopsticks. All kinds of grasses and flowers filled the bowls. Often we got so absorbed in our play that we forgot to return home for lunch. When we grew tired of the dollhouse, we jumped rope or played hide and seek.

At New Year's, we jumped on the New Year see-saw board, each of us dressed in her most colorful *cho-gori*, the top part of a Korean woman's dress, and *chima*, the skirt. My sisters, cousins, and friends took turns at this game. As we jumped on the see-saw board the bright red ribbons at the end of our pigtails, and our green or blue skirts floated up and down in the air. When we were up high, we could look over the wall where neighbors would be watching us. On the other hand, boys in their holiday clothes took to the hillsides and flew kites as their New Year sport. Their kites sometimes flew right over us and we got all excited trying to catch them.

A similar celebration took place every year in late spring when Swing Day, the fifth of May according to our lunar calendar, came round. The girls with their black pigtails tied with red ribbons and wearing colorful dresses of red, blue, green, yellow, and pink, swung in and out gracefully. Being the youngest girl, I never had really new dresses. Mine were always hand-me-downs and made-over ones. But they were always good enough for me and I was contented in them.

One year, I remember, mother had a bright pink *cho-gori* and a pretty green *chima* made over for me. After the morning wash on New Year's Day she was handing out to each of us a bundle of our New Year clothes. When my turn came, the brothers began to tease me again. "Your clothes are only made-over ones.

You don't really belong to our family. Somebody cast you away and mother picked you up under a bridge." I looked at mother and her smile assured me that they were talking nonsense. Anyway the colors were excitingly pretty and I was as happy and proud as a peacock all through the holiday season. Mother told me years later that from that time on she knew she could always depend upon me. This understanding and trust were, of course, mutual and lasted as long as she lived.

There were many more happy events and seasons during my childhood. Near the stream in front of our house was our neighborhood well from which we drew our drinking water. Women, like many across the world, filled up their earthen jars and carried them on their heads. This was a job for grown-ups, but I wanted so much to share it and asked mother to let me try. I was overwhelmed when mother told me I could and gave me a miniature earthen jar she had bought for me. I carried the water on my head all afternoon until I filled up the big jar in our kitchen. My joy and satisfaction over this accomplishment were complete.

Mother was very religious, always praying for the welfare of her family and friends. My father showed his religion in a very different way. He was primarily concerned with ancestral worship according to the Confucian teachings. Our ancestral tablets with names, titles, and important dates written on them were reverently kept in a specially prepared shrine placed at the most central and sacred location.

On the anniversary of the birth or death of each ancestor, special sacrifices were offered. Mother would get the food ready, but it was father who performed the ceremony of sacrifice. The tablet of the particular ancestor to be honored would be set up on the center of a high table with candles on each side and an incense burner in front. On a lower table the prepared food would be laid out. Then father would appear wearing new mourning clothes. All the male members stood behind him and made three bows together to the spirit of the ancestor. Female members of the household were not allowed to participate in this ceremony. Then father would read from his scroll a newly written message to the spirit of the ancestor. After the scroll was read, it was burned and three more bows were made. Then the tablet was put back into the shrine, and the shrine moved back to its permanent place.

As the master of the household, father was always meticulous about these ceremonies. But he left placating of the other household gods to mother, as most men did and still do today. Confucianism is recognized in Korea as an ethical system rather than a religion. There are elements of ancestor worship which are akin to religion, but this is in reality more a veneration of the culture heritage of one's ancestors. That is why when you ask members of a family controlled by the teachings of Confucius what their religion is, they rarely mention Confucianism. They say they have no religion.

On the other hand, mother had embraced animism as her religion, as did many other women of her generation. A form of animistic nature worship was the earliest indigenous religion of the Korean people and has continued to play an important role in Korean culture. Mother believed that there were spirits of the household, as well as of the mountains, waters, stones, and other natural objects. She worshiped and offered regular sacrifices to the nature spirits. She would go to the mountains or to a cold spring in summertime where she would fold her hands and usually make three bows,

8

worshiping the spirits of the mountains and of the water.

Mother believed that the household spirits controlled the welfare of her family, and that she must worship and make sacrifices often enough to appease them and hold their favor. In our main living room she had a special chest on a shelf in which she kept the paraphernalia belonging to the Spirit of Welfare. I remember that this chest contained a whole outfit of costly fabrics for a gentleman's wear. In the storeroom she kept a straw-made image representing the Spirit of Provision. This idol was kept in a miniature earthen shrine with a thatched roof over it. In the room right by the gateway in the outer wall, she kept a box on a shelf containing colorful clothes and weapons for the Spirit of Protection. Mother's religious life and thought were dominated by fear.

In later years she told some fantastic stories of this period of her life. One year she designated for future use as a sacrifice to the Spirit of Protection a certain one of the twelve baby pigs she was raising. That particular pig grew especially fast. One afternoon some friends came to visit, looked over the litter of pigs, and pointed out to mother how big and fat that particular pig was. They remarked that it could be sold for a good price. Mother was raising these pigs to supplement the family budget and agreed that she might change her plan and sell it for that purpose. When she went to feed the pigs the next morning, she found that special pig with jaws closed tight, unable to eat.

In the practice of animistic worship, when there had been no time for preparation of foods for sacrifice, one usually used a table with a clean dish of pure water. Mother quickly set a table with a dish of pure water on it and went down on her knees before the spirit and

9

begged for forgiveness. In prayer she told him that if he would forgive her and restore the health of the pig, she would surely use it for sacrifice to him. The pig got well and mother carried out her promise. There were other stories like this which showed that mother was held in constant fear of unseen spirits.

But a change was to take place in mother's religion. A certain elderly lady, Mrs. Helen Kim, had been making frequent calls on mother. She was a sweet and gentle person with poise and quiet manners. She and mother developed a genuine friendship. Mrs. Kim was a visiting Bible woman who assisted the pastor of the Christian church. The pastor, being a man, could not visit the women in their homes. As mother became friendly with Mrs. Kim and heard from her about the Christian message, she became an earnest seeker after the truths of the Christian religion. She began to see for herself the difference between the spirits she feared and the God that her friend believed to be her loving Father. Mother never hesitated to change whenever she found a better way. Being true to herself, she decided to embrace the Christian religion and to leave the other spirits alone.

Having left this domain to mother and seeing the favorable change in her, father readily agreed to have the family become Christian. His only remaining concern was, "What about the ancestral worship?" Early Protestant churches in Korea declared ancestral worship an idolatry and forbade their members to continue the practice. Father, like other men, did not feel it right to forsake his ancestors in order to become a Christian. So father talked about it with mother and decided that they would give up all forms of idolatry in ancestral worship, which the church rightly condemned. But the

10

spirit of reverence toward the ancestors and the memory of their noble deeds would be kept alive in the family. Instead of the old idolatrous method of ancestral worship, we always had Christian memorial services on the ancestral dates.

The Sunday after mother and father made their decision, all the members of the family formally attended church. After the morning service they were accompanied home by the Bible woman, the pastor, and some other officers of the church. Then out from the gatehouse came the God of Protection with all his regalia. From the shelf in the living room came the chest of fine clothes belonging to the Spirit of Welfare. Out from the storehouse came the straw image of the Spirit of Provision, along with his earthen shrine. The feet of mother and my sisters were swift and sure bringing out the questionable images and boxes from all corners of the house. At last father and the pastor came slowly and with dignity, bringing even the tablets of family ancestors from the shrine. The pile in the center of our courtyard was completed and we all stood in a circle watching the fire burning up all the idols. As the fire died, the pastor held a service. Several hymns of faith and victory were sung, Scriptures read, testimonies given, and prayers offered. It was a never-to-be-forgotten experience.

Mother told us that after this experience those spirits which used to bother her and kept her in constant fear never came near her. They did not appear to her even in her dreams because, she said, "I have found the only true God and have become His child. He protects me with His power and love. They dare not come near and bother me any more."

Mother, like many other women who changed their

11

faith from animism to Christianity, never quite made the complete transfer from the conception of many spirits to monotheism. However, this does not imply that their faith in God, the loving Father, was any weaker than the faith of those well versed in theology. As far as I can remember, ever since mother became a Christian, there was a change in her general attitude toward life. I was too young to know her inner transformation, but it was on the outside; I could tell she was different. She repeatedly said to many that she had been dominated too long by fear; but after she found God and knew for herself that she was the child of a loving Father, there was no more fear in her life.

We saw that mother was depending upon her loving heavenly Father all the time, and her prayer life was almost constant. There were formal times in the evening before we went to bed and in the morning after we got up when mother would try to assemble us and have family prayers, and then she offered her own individual prayers as she went to bed and as she rose in the morning. But these were more or less routine prayers. As I remember now, her life was a life of constant prayer. Often I would see her by the side of a wall in a quiet place, or working in the kitchen, or just sitting, with her two hands folded and her lips moving in prayer. Sometimes in moments of sudden emergencies she would exclaim, saying, "Father, help me!" or "Help us!"

Six months after the burning of the idols, on a Sunday morning in 1905, mother had the whole family dressed up in new clothes. My baby brother and I were too young to understand, but all the older members had had consultations and seemed to realize what was going to take place. We were ushered into the big brick church, the first and the largest Methodist church in Inchon.

We were all seated on the floor in one row near the front; but my father and brothers were on the men's side, while mother and my sisters and I were on the women's side. In the olden days curtains divided the two; but on this Sunday there were no curtains, we just had to sit on our respective sides. I remember a strange looking man with a very high nose and deep eyes on the platform, and a still queerer looking woman with light complexion, yellow hair, and very blue eyes. I could not make out what they were and I could not ask mother any questions, for the atmosphere was one of reverence and she had warned me beforehand to be very quiet. Both my baby brother and I behaved very well, to mother's content.

After a while there was a stir all around and people in white clothes were coming up to the front of the church. The strange looking lady came to mother and spoke in Korean, telling her to go up to the altar. Father and my brothers came from the men's side and mother from the women's, with all her daughters. Our family was joined together in a row facing the altar. Pretty soon the man with the high nose stood in front of me saying something I could not understand and sprinkling water over my head, as he did to all the others in the row. I felt that something very serious was happening to me. Mother told me later that we were all baptized. Mother and father had dedicated themselves and all the rest of us to God. From that time on we belonged to God as His children. I accepted it all then and never thought of anything else.

Right from the time she was converted mother was out doing personal evangelism. One of the stories I love to tell when I go around preaching in churches is how, in my young days, mother would get us ready to go to

13

church. She would give us clean clothes and would see that we were all washed, and that each of us had a Bible and hymn book and our collection money. But there was another thing she would do—she would take one convert to her church every Sunday. She herself had met Christ, not through a Pauline type of experience, but through the day-by-day personal witness of the Bible woman. And that was the way mother shared her faith with others. Each week for the remainder of her life she sought to lead one person to Christ.

With baptism, mother and the younger children got new names. A new life began with the new names, especially for the female folk who, as I have explained before, were not important enough to have their own personal names. Actually, I had been given a name, but nothing so good that I needed to keep it. So we were all given new names. Dr. Cable, the minister, accidentally exchanged the names chosen for mother and me when we were baptized. So mother was Mrs. Dora Pak Kim ever after and I got the name of Helen, which I liked much better as I grew up. Even my Korean name Kideuk was changed to Whallan, which means "living orchid." The professional namers, with all their knowledge of the signs of the zodiac, say that they could not have improved on my name. Everybody in Korea calls me Kim Whallan, while friends abroad know me as Helen Kim.

The Reverend Cable, who baptized us, and Miss Miller, who helped mother to become a Christian, were the first Westerners that our family learned to know and respect. So baptism brought the first contact with Western people as well as with Christian culture, which gave me insight into the possibilities of human life at its highest level and the motivation to pursue it with all my being. But this was for me to discover gradually in subsequent years.

Another revolutionary event that took place at home was sending my sisters to school. When mother heard about the possibility, she was almost as happy as when she first heard about the church. Mother had had to struggle for her own education. Except among the elite families, girls of mother's day were not supposed to learn to read and write. Boys must be taught the arts and letters, but not girls. Household skills were considered sufficient education for girls, who were usually taught by their mothers in the home. But women like my mother had a great yearning for education and did almost anything to learn. Some girls stole their education, hiding behind the screen while their brothers were being taught by hired teachers.

Mother had struggled all alone for her education. A family friend knew her longing and brought her a copy of the Korean alphabet. Mother virtually devoured it. The Korean language is easy to learn to read and write from the alphabet. An eager and intelligent mind like mother's was able to learn and comprehend it without the assistance of a teacher. But mother's father was so violently against her learning to read that she had to hide her text in his presence. She could study only after he had gone away. Many times she was found studying and punished by him severely, but she never gave up. Somehow she mastered the art of reading and read everything she could get hold of. She became a person of considerable culture and understanding. When she found that she could send her daughters to Christian schools, she remembered her own struggles and sufferings. She was glad that a new day had arrived for girls and lost no time in sending all her daughters to school.

15

In seizing this new opportunity, she was vicariously fulfilling her own aspirations.

My two stepsisters were older and had already married. The next ones, my favorite sister Ellen, and Marion, were too big to be seen on the streets walking back and forth between our home and the girls' school near our church in Inchon. In those days teen-age girls were not allowed to be seen on the streets unless they wore full capes covering them from head to foot. Only one eye could peep out to see where they were going. It made no difference how long or short the distances were. Often they went in covered carriage chairs. So my sisters were sent up to Seoul and put into a boarding school, Ewha Haktang, an unclassified school for girls, the very first school for girls in all Korea. It was founded by Mrs. Mary F. Scranton, the first missionary of the Woman's Foreign Missionary Society of the Methodist Episcopal Church of the United States.

I was small enough to walk on the streets alone and with nothing over my head, so mother sent me to Young-Wha, the girls' school in Inchon. I enjoyed the freedom of going back and forth to school, and the things I learned at the school were fascinating: the Korean alphabet, Chinese characters, Arabic numerals, songs and stories. In the evenings I made detailed reports to mother as to what I had learned. She always had a contented look on her face, and the light of joy in her eyes gave me great encouragement. In her evening prayers she would thank God for giving her daughters the privilege of learning, which had been denied to her. Her prayers for her two daughters in Ewha and for the one in Young-Wha were always, "Father, help them to become better servants of Thine than their mother could ever be."

On Sunday mornings the family all got up early to go to church. Mother took my older brother John, baby Paul, and me to Sunday school. The Bible stories and children's hymns we learned were so interesting and stimulating that sometimes we went about the rest of the day singing or repeating them.

At Christmas time the Sunday school usually gave a program at the church. Our Sunday school teachers usually asked us to do anything we could do well, whether it had anything to do with Christmas or not. One year Mr. Choi, the superintendent, asked me to tell the Korean tale of the donkey egg. The story went something like this: "One winter night a poor old childless couple huddled together in a warm spot on the floor trying to go to sleep. A peddler went by their window saying, 'Someone please buy my donkey egg. It will be hatched tonight if kept in a warm spot.' The old couple were curious and decided to buy it. They laid the egg on the warmest spot between them, covered it up with layers of cotton, and tried to add the warmth of their bodies to it. Soon after midnight they were startled by the loud and sudden cracking of the shell. Lo and behold, not a donkey but a beautiful child rose out of the shell! Making a deep bow, the child called them Father and Mother. With great joy the old couple thanked the heavens for sending them a son."

This story went well on the program and I was asked to tell it many times in other gatherings. One day some of us from the Sunday school were escorted to the big house of the mayor of Inchon. He had an elegant home with expensive furniture. He and his family gathered round. Mr. Choi directed us in singing songs and telling stories. I was asked to repeat the donkey egg story. The

17

mayor was very much pleased and gave us tea and cookies to eat and presents to take with us. The gift for me was a family of toy chickens: a hen, rooster, and six little chicks. This was the first manufactured toy I had ever had and the chicken family occupied an important place in my dollhouse, where I had made everything out of scraps.

My first experience of real sadness took place when I was seven years old. In November 1905, following the Russo-Japanese War, Japan had established a protectorate over Korea and assumed almost complete control of public functions. One evening after supper my parents talked about the departure of our nine-year-old Prince Eun Li from Inchon harbor. He had been taken away by force as a hostage by Japanese officers. He struggled and refused to go. As he was torn away from his family and taken up to the boat, he was so brokenhearted and cried out so desperately to his mother that everybody at the harbor cried with him.

As I heard this account, something began to stir within me. Tears flowed and would not stop all night long. I felt so sorry for him and so rebellious against the Japanese who had taken him by force from his mother, his family, his home, and his country. I had not seen the event at the harbor, but the picture was vivid in my mind. Although too young to understand all the political implications, the feeling of cruelty and injustice involved was too sharp and deep ever to be forgotten.

Prince Eun Li returned to Korea recently as an invalid with his Japanese wife and a son, who had married an American girl while he was studying in the United States. As we know the story, the prince was held in Japan and was given a Japanese education. The Japanese tried to erase his Korean nationality by marrying him into a Japanese family, but we know he kept up his Korean spirit and remained a Korean. Our people have received him well, and he and his family seem to be very happy.

II

STUDENT DAYS

From the year 1906, father's business had many reverses and mother's supplementary projects did not bring in adequate income to depend upon. Our family life could not be maintained and something had to be done. Because of her strong desire to educate us, mother took the initiative and decided to move up to Seoul.

Of course this decision was made with father's full consent. He saw that there was not much future for the family in Inchon and agreed to our moving to Seoul, although he could not join us for the time being. He had to stay on in Inchon and carry on his business in order to support the family of his oldest son, my stepbrother, who had left the farm and followed father to Inchon, bringing his whole family of seven. He never made a living for himself or for his family on the farm or in the city. On the contrary he caused only difficulties in father's business. But father never complained, and helped him and his family even with the last earnings of his life. He depended upon mother's resourcefulness and industry to maintain our end of the family up in Seoul.

Mother's determination was to find for us in Seoul an opportunity for the best possible education. In the spring of 1907 the entire family took the train and in an hour arrived at the Seoul station. We were breaking away from the old homestead, but mother was brave and adventurous and I did not know enough to feel sad. I was only nine years old. It was my first train ride, so everything was exciting and I felt gay all through the trip. Mother had given me the responsibility of taking care of one of our bundles, and even though my eyes were constantly looking for new and interesting sights both within and outside the train, I never let the bundle out of my hands.

Mother led us all to a house she had already rented in a poor section of the city. It was by an open canal just beyond Ha-Kyo bridge. The house had several rooms, because mother's plan was to take in boarders. The house itself compared favorably with the old home in Inchon, but it did not begin to have the spacious courtyard and the grand view of the sweep of field and stream, of mountain and hillside that we loved so much.

As soon as some order was established in our new home, mother took me to Ewha Haktang. I remember that the Ewha students called the campus their "Ewha Garden of Pear Blossoms." In this garden I was given a good start as one of the smallest pear trees. My two sisters were already boarding there. Mother could not pay my board and since I was still small enough, I walked back and forth to school as I had done in Inchon. Here at the school I found my second home, with a great deal of space and with all the playmates I needed. Every morning before school and each afternoon after lessons, Bessie Lim and Qui-up Kim and I had the time of our lives on the playground, playing hide and seek, hopscotch, and jumping the rope.

One day when I returned home later than usual after having played overtime, mother welcomed me in a very unusual manner. She was in the kitchen with a stick to poke the fire when I entered the gate. She greeted me with a whack with that stick and scolded me for coming home late when she needed me so badly at home. She was almost crying. I felt surprised and sorry. So I rushed about and tried to help with the household chores, feeling that mother's trouble was not just my being late. She calmed down very quickly, but was very quiet and serious all through the evening meal.

Family conversation after the meal revealed that everything had gone wrong that day and that mother was facing a serious problem financially. Later in the evening her special and tender attention reassured me of her love. This was the only time mother had ever been angry with me or given me a whipping. As a matter of fact, my married sisters had always complained about mother's laxity with my discipline compared to her former sternness with them. Mother would always say, "But she is a good girl; I don't need to scold or punish her."

Mother's financial affairs were going from bad to worse and she could no longer afford to keep both of my sisters in the dormitory. At the same time, the school was getting so crowded that the administration felt the need of screening the students. In this process sister Marion had to leave, for she just could not make the grades. For sister Ellen, mother had to face a choice between marriage and further studies. Ellen's teachers at school had praised her work highly and had planned for her further studies abroad. Miss Lulu E. Frey, our Principal, recognized her leadership qualities and wanted her to take further training instead of getting married. On the other hand, a middleman had been coming to Ellen and to mother bringing an urgent request for marriage from a would-be groom. As was usual in such cases, there was no romance on the part of either party; but out of pure calculation the request was sent and received. After days of indecision both mother and

Ellen, considering her age and our family financial condition, decided in favor of the wedding.

My mother was determined for me to continue in school, but she felt that I was getting too big now to walk back and forth. So she took this problem to Miss Frey. One day after school our class teacher called the names of three of us and took us to the Principal's office. We did not know what was going to happen and were very much afraid. We had seen Miss Frey from a distance when she led chapel exercises but never had been close to her. She was tall and had deep blue eyes and curly hair. But her nose was not so big or so prominent as that of other Westerners. Among ourselves we used to whisper that our Principal could pass as an Oriental if we looked at her nose only. There was no definite reason for us to be afraid of her, but we were. Partly it was because we were taught to stay away from our superiors and elders out of respect, which was almost synonymous with fear.

When my turn came, Miss Frey motioned to me, looking at me through her glasses. She asked my name and then said, "Do you like your studies?" "Yes," was my quick reply. Then she pulled me still closer to her saying, "Don't be afraid." She looked at me closely. I was almost trembling by this time. Then nodding her head and smiling, she told me I could leave. The next day our class teacher told me that Miss Frey had decided to take me as a scholarship student and that I was to come into the dormitory that weekend.

Mother was very happy at the news and made preparations. She provided bedding, towels, a washbasin, a set of rice and soup bowls with spoon and chopsticks, all new, and a chest for my clothes and other private belongings. It was necessary for mother to hire a man with an A-frame. The customary way to carry a heavy burden upon one's back is to use this wooden frame, made into the shape of the letter A. Two sticks protruding out several inches in the middle support and keep the burden in place. The A-frame is still used all over Korea.

So the man with my baggage on his A-frame, mother, and I walked together one Saturday afternoon to the dormitory. The matron and the "big sister" of the room to which I was assigned met us. I had been to this dormitory before to see sister Ellen and everything had looked very nice and cozy then. But this time when I came there to live, things looked different. Mother left me in good hands, but that first night, sleeping in strange surroundings and away from mother, I was painfully lonesome. Homesick tears flowed down upon my pillow much of the night.

Soon I got used to the dormitory life. My roommates became good friends and we loved our big sister. She was Eva Syn who had been a devoted friend of my sister Ellen. She took me as her responsibility. Over every weekend I had to wash my dress for the coming week. Eva Syn usually helped me, often doing the actual work herself.

My dress used to be colorful, a bright pink *cho-gori* with green or blue *chima,* or vice versa. The material was of cotton cloth. In wintertime the *cho-gori* was padded with a layer of cotton for warmth. After a week's wear I had to take the outside and the lining apart before washing them. Usually the outside material had to be re-dyed. After the material had been washed and dyed, I had to go through the process of ironing by beating it with two round sticks on a large flat stone. This process not only ironed but also added glaze and

24

stiffness to the material. Then I rolled the material over a large round post and beat it again to take out the stiffness and add more glaze. The sound of this ironing is rhythmical when you hear it from a distance. Poets have written about the music of this sound coming through the paper windows of a country home from which shines the dim light of a kerosene lamp.

After the ironing was finished, I had to sew the different parts together again, with the layer of cotton in between. This was my usual weekend chore.

For my weekly hot bath Eva Syn carried water from the big caldron on the lower level of the kitchen up to the adjoining bathroom where wooden tubs were placed in corners behind curtains. When I protested, she always said that I was too small to carry the heavy bucket full of water and that she was doing it for me in place of my sister Ellen. Whenever she had some extra candy or fruit she never forgot me. While I ate heartily she would pat my back and smile, her love shining out of her tiny bright eyes.

Bessie and Qui-up were also living in the dormitory and we three became inseparable playmates. There was no corner around the buildings on the compound where our feet did not reach for play and mischief.

Our mood of play was extended into the classrooms. One of the teachers in Chinese classics had a small tumor on top of his head, which was mostly bald. His nickname was Hok-boori, tumor pinnacle. One afternoon after assigning us a lesson, he told us to study and memorize it, then sat down and began to nod his head from sleepiness. It was too good a chance! The three of us got together quickly, rolled and folded a small piece of paper and threw it at the "tumor pinnacle." We made it and the class roared with laughter as he

25

touched his head with his startled hand. We should have been punished but he just smiled and dismissed the class. For the following days we three culprits were expecting discipline from some source but it never came.

However, much play and little work brought down our grades to a dangerous level. I barely escaped failing that year. This taught me a lesson and I began to do some serious work.

While I was vacationing at my sister Ellen's home during the summer of 1910, the terrible woe fell upon us. On the twenty-ninth of August the annexation of Korea to Japan was announced. My brother-in-law, Dal-Ha Kim, had gone to his office in the Government. He came back early in the afternoon and he went straight to his room, tore off his official garments and knelt by his desk, wailing. In our own places and rooms, sitting or standing, the entire household, including callers, wept with him bitterly. Suddenly a friend came in from the streets saying, "Stop crying and be quiet." He said that our army had gone to the mountains for guerrilla warfare, refusing to be disarmed, and that the police and gendarmes were everywhere, watching and arresting rebellious citizens. We should not make so much noise.

From that day on we had no freedom even to weep when we felt like it; and devotion for our country and our people, oppressed and suppressed by an alien power, took deep roots within my being. With patriotism, hatred and bitterness for anything Japanese grew side by side, until only a supernatural Power could help me to overcome it years later. There is nothing worse that could happen to any people than to be enslaved and subjugated by another people. The effect of the national tragedy of 1910 was like casting a black veil over the heads of the entire people throughout the whole peninsula.

Young as well as old felt the curse of this great evil. Our hearts were sore, but we could go on to school. Continuing in our studies helped us to maintain steady nerves and high hopes for the future. Within us the determination to study well and work hard to free our people grew stronger and stronger. By the time I graduated from the secondary department of Ewha Haktang in 1913, this serious purpose for life was well established. After graduation I hoped to go right on through the college preparatory year and then on to the regular four-year college course.

My father had a long illness that year and we were not sure that he was out of danger the day I graduated. When I visited him at his sickbed and told him I was planning to go to college, he said emphatically, "No!" In his physical weakness he lapsed back into the old conservative world of ideas and customs. He said I was already of marriageable age and going to school for five more years was unthinkable; I should stay at home and become skilled in household arts in preparation for marriage. Unless I obeyed him, he said, I was no longer his daughter or he my father. What a crisis this presented! How could I disobey the stern command of father on his sickbed? On the other hand, how could I stop going to school when I was just beginning to experience the enriching influence of education?

My determination to prepare myself through education to serve my people and my nation was getting stronger every day. The marriage problem father spoke of had not occurred to my mind in the least. The overall life purpose, already well established in my consciousness, was a sweepingly great one; and the question

27

of marriage had no chance to attract my attention. Having had no contacts with any male outside of my family, there had been no occasion for encountering a real experience of falling in love, which might have posed an actual problem of choice between career and marriage to me. Only the one road of further studies and on to a life of service was open to me, and I decided to take it.

At this time serious minded students were convinced that the way to become equipped to serve our country was through education. We were moved by our purpose to help free our country from the domination of an alien government, and we felt at the same time that this was also the purpose of God for our people. To serve our country and to serve God seemed to be one and the same in our aspirations and in our efforts.

Father did not understand the new position a girl could take in Korea, and I could not argue with him in his weakness. Even so, I was torn to pieces as I thought of disobeying my father. Mother saw the struggle within me, the choice between the old way of absolute obedience to father and the new way of following one's own conscience, even in the case of a daughter. She came to the rescue. She took me to another room and told me that father would think differently when he got his strength back; she would make it all right with him. "Go ahead with your studies. You are the youngest daughter, and there is no one after you to be held up in marriage. If that is your teachers' advice, and you want it, there is no reason why you shouldn't go to college." Relieved and comforted by mother, I went back to school the next day.

During the year something decisive happened to my soul. As mother used to say, I was ordinarily a good girl.

Mother at home and the wonderful missionary teachers at school had never neglected my Christian upbringing. I was one of a small group of ten or twelve girls who had met with a teacher in a King's Daughters Circle every Sunday morning. This was followed by Sunday school, morning and evening worship, and other services throughout the week. Every year after Christmas vacation some famous preacher came and held special religious services. Through the years I had observed these religious practices but they held no special meaning or significance for me. Without my realizing it, my religion was a nominal acceptance of a set of frozen dogmas and was expressed in a routine of lifeless exercises.

This year when the preacher asked us to confess our sins, I began to feel rebellious. Why was he taking us all as sinners? I had no sin to confess. I had done no stealing, no lying, and no injustice to anyone. On the other hand, as he kept telling us we must confess our sins and be pardoned and that we would know our sins if we prayed, I felt disturbed both in mind and heart and lost the sense of security and poise I had had hitherto. At last I could stand it no longer. I either had to get at the reality of religion or else give up altogether the meaningless and therefore hypocritical observances of religious practices.

At this point I remembered and took the preacher's suggestion and began to pray as I had never prayed before. I asked God, if He existed, to reveal to me the truth concerning what the preacher, His messenger, told us—that we were all sinners who must be redeemed by Christ. I struggled and prayed this prayer all night long. Suddenly the illumination came to me that my sins were pride, self-will, and hatred for the Japanese. I fell upon the floor and asked God to forgive all my

29

sins committed against Him. I immediately felt His forgiveness. This was followed by a remarkable vision. I seemed to see Him take the three bags of my sins away, showing me what to do the rest of my life. He pointed out to me a big dug-out moat where a mass of Korean women were crying out for help with their hands outstretched from the haze and confusion that covered them. The whole vision was very real to me. This must have been what is usually called a spiritual awakening. From that time on, my life has been directed by God's hand toward the one course of humble service to the womanhood of my country and the emancipation of the women of the world. I could ask of my religion no other reality than His presence with me throughout life.

After such an experience, the different studies at school began to be more interesting and stimulating than before. Geology and astronomy opened up a new world full of wonder and amazement. Geometry and trigonometry gave me the sheer joy of conquering the unknown. When I asked what followed in this field my teacher's answer was calculus. I wanted to study that. Miss Frey was wiser and said, "No, you have had enough in mathematics. You should sample other areas of knowledge." I was introduced to chemistry and physics, music, art, and some household skills. I liked music so much that I wanted to go ahead and continue its study, but our favorite and only teacher suddenly left to be married and we had no more music lessons for a long time.

We had a little bit of many things, but our major course was English language and literature taught by American teachers. The language was hard but not impossible to learn. The literature was difficult to understand because our historical background and social customs were so different from those depicted in the English classics, both prose and poetry. Our study of European and American history was a great revelation of a part of the world which we had not known much about before. We were denied formal studies in Korean history by the Japanese authorities.

At the close of my college preparatory year, in the spring of 1914, an historic event took place in Chung Dong church—our leading Methodist church in Seoul. The occasion was Ewha's first college graduation.

I sat among Ewha students watching breathlessly as the first three women college graduates marched in wearing caps and gowns. Alice Kim, Marsook Syn, and Dorothy Lee made up the trio of graduates. Everyone was proud of them as potential leaders in the nation. The audience rose and stood in silence. It was a scene that had never before taken place in Korea. For girls to go to college and graduate and enter into professions was an unheard of thing. As the three girls took their seats on the platform and so ably performed throughout the commencement exercises, thrills ran up and down my back and tears rolled down upon my cheeks. I looked around and saw that others were crying too, even some men. These were tears of joy for the accomplishments of girls so long neglected and looked down upon. There was rejoicing over the fact that Korean women were proving that they too are capable of higher education, and of realizing opportunities for better life and greater achievements.

Everyone present felt the unexpressed nationalistic aspiration that all the youth of Korea, girls and boys, would receive higher education and someday throw off the burden of colonial power. For us no experience of any significance ever transpired without being connected

31

psychologically with the sad and bitter fact of an alien rule.

We all admired and loved Miss Lulu Frey for the courageous stand she was taking on our behalf. Miss Frey was the person who had had the vision of a woman's college in Korea. In spite of opposition she had held on to her vision and had worked to fulfill it.

In 1915, when I was in the sophomore class, our total college enrollment was only five—two freshmen, one sophomore, one junior, and one senior. In my own class, four of us had started together, but in a year or two the others dropped out on account of health or marriage. This gave good support to those opposed to Miss Frey's efforts to build up a college for women in Korea. Even some of her missionary associates argued that the time was not yet ripe for a woman's college. Why should the time of so many teachers be wasted on such a small group? It would be better to concentrate on the hundreds and thousands of children not yet even in the primary grades.

Miss Frey held her ground. She was so right in her persistent idea that Korean women leaders were needed in all fields, and that they should be trained in Korea. She had already tried training a few by sending them abroad, and knew from experience that the better way was to do it within their own country. So she stood firm against all opposition and obstacles and carried on with a handful of students. Gradually the enrollment increased, and for thirty years, a whole generation, Ewha College served the women of Korea as the only institution of higher education for women.

The dreams of Miss Frey inspired others, and young women from the United States volunteered to come to Ewha as teachers. The first three were Jeannette Walter,

Olive Pye, and Grace Harmon. Their arrival meant a new program and a new life for our college. A vigorous program of physical culture was started. Regular gymnastic exercises, tennis, basketball for girls! These were revolutionary steps. Our skirts which had been tied tightly around our chests by long bands were now suspended from loose bodices to hang from the shoulders. This gave room for our breathing organs to grow and expand. Skirts were shortened, freeing our legs to walk and run naturally. We were enthusiastic over everything that these new young teachers taught, and physical freedom was thoroughly enjoyed through all kinds of sports, games, and drills.

I became very sick that winter with a severe case of pleurisy. This presented a serious problem to my teachers. If I had to drop out of school, a whole class would vanish. Not only for my sake, but for the college as well, the entire staff worked hard to restore my health. Miss Walter, who was in charge of the health program, helped to nurse me day and night, while Dr. Van Buskirk, a wonderful missionary doctor at Severance Hospital, gave all the necessary treatments to help me. In time I did get better and returned to classes but remained an invalid all through the term, for the illness had affected my lungs and left me weak and sickly. The doctor ruled out all physical exertion. No more sports and exercise in the gymnasium were allowed.

All the scholarship students were assigned some work in the dormitory. I could still wait at the tables one day a week, but was not allowed to do any heavy cleaning. Instead, the teachers gave me the responsibility of ringing the bell—at five thirty in the morning, for every class hour during the day, three times a day for meals, for evening study hours, and at ten at night for going to bed. It was sad to give up the joy of physical activities, but through this adversity I gained to a certain degree the habit of punctuality.

Fresh air and good food were the other two orders from the doctor. These were difficult to obtain in dormitory life. The food in the dormitory was good, but not adequate for an invalid. Ordinarily five or six girls slept together in one small room and the air could not stay fresh very long. Miss Walter with her ingenuity soon devised ways and means. To supplement the food, she ordered our dormitory nurse, Mrs. Hanna Park, to give me two soft-boiled eggs every morning. At night she had me come down to her kitchen and eat an extra bowl of hot soup before going to bed. This was the kitchen for the missionary teachers who lived in one of the wings of the main hall.

For fresh air she set up a cot on a small side porch with a southeast exposure. There were doors out from her bedroom and from Miss Frey's. She had me sleep there the year round, with heavy bedding and hot water bottles in winter. Miss Frey's room was nearest to our dormitory, so I went to bed through her room and out to the porch. When coughing spells attacked me, Miss Walter used to come out of her room and help relieve the strain. Under such love and care I had every chance to rebuild good health as well as to continue my studies.

Like many others in their late teens, I began to think over questions about life and death and their meaning. The first time I faced this big problem was at the death of my little brother from diphtheria. This occurred a year before my illness. For days I could not stand the thought of my brother being laid away in the cold ground. Then in a few months my sister Marion died after giving birth to her first son. These two tragedies in my family made me think seriously for the first time about life and death. Mother was very brave and told me not to grieve. When I asked her "What is death?" her answer was, "When Confucius was asked the same question he said, 'Man does not know what life is, how can he know what death is?' " Then she added, "God knows best and they are in His hands. We need only believe and wait for the day we meet them again in heaven." Mother's words and attitude toward this family tragedy helped me to accept it without further questions, but I was determined to find out in time the why of suffering and death.

The outbreak of World War I in 1914 was another reason why so many students tended to become serious. It was true that we were far away from the actual scenes, but every bit of news was absorbed. Even in my immature mind questions arose again and again: Why would intelligent men go to war on such a big scale? Couldn't they settle their disputes by negotiations or by legal procedures? Why would civilized and, furthermore, so-called Christian nations resort to force, killing off each other instead of sitting around a table and calmly talking through and resolving their differences? What is the real meaning of civilization? Is there any difference between the Christian and non-Christian nations? Is Western civilization as seen through this war what we really want? Such questions kept rising in our minds all through the war years.

My senior year in the college department began on April 1, 1917. The enrollment at Ewha on the lower and secondary levels was increasing rapidly and the dormitory and classrooms were all full to overflowing. We were crowded everywhere. The college had no building of its own, having been crowded out by large high school classes. College classes met mostly in the bedroom corners of our teachers. But no one complained. We were too grateful for the opportunity to go to college and too happy to be learning something new and interesting every day. My health improved and I was able to ring the bells faithfully.

From the early spring days flowers adorned our campus. Forsythia, azaleas, lilacs, and peonies bloomed in succession and were at their best on May 31, when we had the May Day exercises. This was and still is the great annual event celebrating Founder's Day. Every year we began the May Day celebration with a grand march of the entire student body in white dresses, symbolic of white pear blossoms. This was followed by the crowning of the May Queen. Then all kinds of drills and musical numbers and sometimes scenes from operas or dramas made up the program.

In selecting the May Queen, the senior classes of all the different departments elected their own choices. Then a faculty committee composed of members not belonging to any particular department made the final choice of May Queen from the list of candidates submitted by the students. This year the problem was a grave one, for I was the only college senior. My looks could never fit a May Queen, but the authorities decided to make me one. I had no proper clothes to wear, so Miss Walter went to her Korean friend, Mrs. Mary Sohn, and borrowed a beautiful silk dress of light aquamarine. Somebody else's white shoes were borrowed. Instead of a long Korean braid, my hair was put up in Grecian style. Having been dressed to look like a queen I walked in the long line with a beautiful bouquet in my arms, surrounded by flower maids, and stepped up on the throne to be crowned. Thus I was a May Queen once in my lifetime by virtue of being the only senior!

The summer and autumn months passed by swiftly without very unusual events, and it was possible to concentrate more upon my studies. By this time I found reading in English literature very rewarding. For this purpose the summer vacation was too short. When the winter term began in January 1918 my life purpose was coming into sharper focus in my thinking. I had already joined the small group of student volunteers as one of the initial members. I pledged to go whenever and wherever God wanted me to serve in His name. "Where He leads me, I will follow" was our group song. I had translated it into Korean and we sang it together each time we met, meaning every word in its deepest sense. Graduation was coming the following March, and I knew I was going to follow God's lead. I was so anxious to start on my life of service that I wished the time would fly and bring the graduation time closer.

At this time mother was a Bible woman in much demand. She served in many churches in several districts of the Seoul area. The pay she received was not enough even to pay for the shoes she was wearing out walking all the time over the difficult roads. And it was out of this meager income that she tried to help provide my clothes. My sister Ellen helped some as long as she was in Seoul, but soon after annexation her family had moved to Peking to live in exile. So when graduation came I had no money and no dress for the occasion.

By close inspection of what I had, I found an old cotton dress yellowed with age. Very thorough washing and good ironing made the old dress seem new. Someone asked me whether or not I had a new silk dress! Again my braid of hair had to be put up to go with the cap I was to wear. To match the rest I must have foreign-

37

style shoes, or so everyone advised. As I was pondering how to manage it a friend came to my rescue. She knew about a pair of secondhand shoes I could get and pay for after I began to draw a salary. I seized the chance and agreed to pay in three installments, beginning in April. I had already entered upon a contract to teach at Ewha after graduation. Even the secondhand shoes would cost my full month's salary of seven *yen*. The shoes were decent enough, but were long boots laced up over the ankles. This made it possible to help them stay on but they were very old-fashioned looking even in 1918. However, they were Western shoes and my long dress and academic gown covered them up mostly. So, apparel-wise, I was all ready for commencement day.

Our graduation exercises took place on March 18, 1918, at seven o'clock in the evening. Chung Dong Church was full again. The twenty-seven graduates from high school, seven from the kindergarten normal training school, two from college preparatory, and I from the college marched in. I was the fifth college graduating class. There was not the same thrill that we all experienced at the first commencement five years before, but again we all were conscious of the new dignity and status that women were gaining in Korea. To us who were graduates, it was a very important occasion. A college graduate was expected to deliver a speech. Mine was on the subject "The Relation of Higher Education to the Home." It was given in both the Korean and English languages.

Thus I became a teacher, a career woman, very young and serious minded. The day I had waited for so long had arrived, the day when I could begin to give as I had received. I could love my people and serve my country in reality and not only in thought.

38

III

INDEPENDENCE MOVEMENT
AND AFTERMATH

Mansei! Mansei! Mansei! Men, women, and children were out in the streets of Seoul shouting with uplifted hands. Ten Thousand Years! Long Live Our Korean Independence! It was March first, the day that went down in Korean history as the date of the 1919 Independence Uprising.

Ever since the Japanese annexation in 1910, no Korean had a stronger desire than for his country's independence. Like a leaven this yearning pervaded all of life. In spite of suppression, Korean nationalism grew.

Korean leaders in exile had formed a provisional government in Shanghai and carried on political activities for our independence. Dr. Syngman Rhee was named as the first president of the provisional government. He organized and headed the Korean Commission in Washington, D.C., and tried to keep the Korean issue alive among the political circles of the world. Later he continued to work from his Honolulu base. Organizations of patriotic Koreans were formed everywhere in order to collect funds for the independence movement.

Within Korea itself there was a well organized underground. Professors, church leaders, students, all had a part. In countries where normal conditions exist and the welfare of the nation is in the hands of competent leaders, students do not need to stop their studies and participate to a great extent in national movements. But the situation was different in Korea. Without the advance of higher education, leaders were few. People who had never had educational opportunities looked to the student groups, and the students themselves felt the weight of responsibility for leadership of the people.

So as one who had just graduated from college, I too was involved. In the underground organization I received funds from schools and churchwomen's groups and relayed them to the top level committee, which in turn dispatched the funds for independence activities abroad. My instructions were never to open up and count the money in the packages nor ask the names of those who brought them or of those who took them. To this day I do not know how much money went through my hands, or the names of the ever-changing individuals who brought and took the packages.

We were so absorbed in our own problems that we hardly knew how World War I was progressing. Then late in the fall of 1918 came the news of the Armistice and something about President Wilson's Fourteen Points as the basis for the Armistice. We were not able to get any copies of President Wilson's speech or to comprehend the full intent of all its points; but the two phrases —self-determination of all peoples, strong or weak, and the independence of Poland—were enough to raise our hopes high for our own independence. It seemed that a new world of justice and righteousness had emerged out of the chaos of World War I and that the greatest hero was President Wilson. From grade school children up, all Koreans felt that independence for us also was just around the corner. If only we could make known to the world our desire for independence, we would surely have it.

Our leaders began to get busy. All other organizations having been dissolved by the Japanese, the representatives of religious groups decided to lead the independence movement. Mr. Son Pyung-hi, representing Chundoism; Mr. Ham Tai-young, the Christian churches; and Mr. Paik-Yong-sung, the Buddhists, got together and decided to mobilize the adherents of their respective religions. Leaders in the provinces were contacted, and student and women's underground movements were notified and activated.

Mr. Choi Nam-sun, one of our eminent scholars in the field of Korean history and literature, drafted the Declaration of Independence. Previously the top leaders in their secret meetings had generally agreed on the principles and ideas to be incorporated in the document. So his draft was accepted almost without revision. The principles of nonretaliation and of nonviolence were emphasized. The whole idea was to declare our rights and to appeal to the conscience of the world, including Japan. The thirty-three leaders, led by Mr. Son Pyung-hi, signed the historic document.

At two o'clock in the afternoon of March 1, 1919, these thirty-three representatives met in Tai-Wha Restaurant, located in the very center of the old walled city of Seoul, and held a brief ceremony to emphasize this significant event in Korean history. After the ceremony they telephoned the Japanese police, informing them where they were and what they had done.

Simultaneously in Pagoda Park the student representatives and younger citizens of Seoul met together to announce the Declaration of Independence. Kim Won Pyuk, the student leader, stood out and announced the opening of the solemn occasion and read through the Declaration, followed by three cheers, *Mansei! Mansei! Mansei!* The students started out in orderly fashion to parade through the streets of Seoul. Citizens joined them at every corner waving either the old flags,

41

cherished and hidden away for a long time, or new flags made at the peril of their lives by different underground groups.

At the same hour on the same day similar events proclaiming the Declaration of Independence took place in other parts of Korea—Pyungyang, Hae-ju, Eui-ju, Kil-ju, Won-ju, Chun-ju, Chin-ju, Suh-san. These were followed by similar events in hundreds of towns and in thousands of villages. The movement went like wildfire sweeping over hills and valleys in dry weather.

However, the peaceful and orderly demonstrations of the people were met with bayonets, imprisonment, and torture by the Japanese police and gendarmery. The harmless *mansei* shouts were silenced and the Korean flags were no longer seen on the streets. As far as outward appearances were concerned, Japanese force had succeeded in putting down the Korean independence movement. The leaders were all in prison, or scattered and gone underground. According to the statistics of the Japanese police of that time, more than twenty-three thousand Koreans were killed or wounded, and slightly less than forty-seven thousand were imprisoned. But no amount of pain and suffering could dim the ever shining hope of independence within the hearts and minds of the people, or kill the burning desire to continue to work for it openly or in secret.

At Ewha the big gate had been strongly bolted on the day of the uprising to make it impossible for any students to get out and participate in the street demonstrations. But before noon many were at the gate demanding that the gateman open it for them. As soon as the teachers were aware of this, our Principal and others came and tried to persuade the students not to leave the campus. Persuasion failed and the girls started to force their way out. Miss Frey stood by the bolted gate, facing them with her arms outstretched to make sure that none would pass. "Well, girls, you will go out over my dead body," she said.

When the girls saw how determined Miss Frey was, some of them returned to their rooms in the dormitory, but a few climbed the walls at points not easily visible and went out to join the independence march. In spite of Miss Frey's protest, more and more of the students left to participate in the demonstrations. Many were taken to prison.

In a few days, because of the unsettled conditions, the school was recessed and the girls went home, but not to sit idly. They became leaders of the independence movement up and down the country. One of them was the famous Yu Kwan-soon, only sixteen years old, who died in prison after carrying the movement to her home town, Chi-ryung-ri, and all the surrounding villages. Soon the police suspected and arrested some of the Korean teachers as leaders behind the scenes. Two of them were my closest friends, Miss Induk Pahk and Miss Julia Syn.

After these two friends were taken to prison, I knew that I must go into hiding. My acts, if found out, would result in heavy punishment not only for myself but also for others involved. My health was too poor to survive the tortures and privations of imprisonment, which was sure to come. My friends made arrangements for my escape. At first even my parents did not know where I was. Miss Marie Church, a young missionary teacher, took the responsibility of taking me by ricksha to the home of a secretary of the British Bible Society in Song-wol Dong, a suburb of Seoul.

I was disguised as a traditional sewing woman and

amah. I played with the three small children of the family and attended to their needs. While they were at school I sewed. I do not remember a single thing I made on the sewing machine, for my mind was preoccupied by the activities of the independence movement. Especially burdened was my heart as I kept hearing the news of my friends in prison. They were receiving extra beatings on my account. Through the window where I sat to sew I could see the prison in the distance. The mental agony was almost unendurable. Many a time I sought for the chance to escape and offer myself to the police. It seemed as though suffering in prison with my friends would be light compared to my mental anguish because of the physical comfort I was enjoying at the cost of their added tortures.

My health suffered under the strain, and the old lung trouble returned. My sickness was never diagnosed with the accuracy doctors employ now, but it was considered to be tuberculosis. Miss Church moved me back to the campus and hid me in a room in the empty college building which used to be called Sontag Hotel. She was the only one who knew where I was, bringing my meals and nursing me as much as she could without arousing suspicion. At night the big building seemed bigger and emptier than in the daytime; but I lay there alone, sleeping most of the time and praying when awake. I was able to regain my peace of mind and to leave the care of my friends and the problem of our independence in God's hands.

A secret meeting was arranged with Dr. Van Buskirk, who proved pessimistic concerning my recovery. He had been so successful in treating me before, that I was sure he could help me to get well again. I was disappointed and discouraged when he said that there was no medicine or treatment he could suggest. He was ready to dismiss me when he added, "You might try sunshine. Lie in the sun and let it penetrate into your painful sides." This would be a slow and uncertain process, and during that time I would not be able to do any work. But I had the conviction that God still had work for me to do and that He was not going to let me die. I felt that if I did my part, my health would surely return.

Miss Church could no longer keep me under her care, so mother and father took me to the summer home of their good friends, Mr. and Mrs. Chang, in Sung-puk Dong, a hilly suburb of Seoul. There was an orchard on the sloping side of the garden facing southeast. It was early in May and the sun was beginning to be warm. Every morning after breakfast my parents carried me a little way up the slope and had me lie there taking the sunbath as long as I could stand it. Mother looked after the housekeeping and cooked different dishes for me to try. We were still a poor family and could not afford any outside help. So father was my nurse, a surprisingly good one. All the little details he anticipated and attended to for my comfort were beyond my expectations. Such tender love and care and the daily sunbath changed the course of my illness. Slowly but surely my appetite came back and strength returned. At the end of five months I was a different person.

All through my illness I never felt impatience or complained, because I knew there was some lesson I needed to learn through this experience. I felt peace in my heart and was confident that everything was in God's hands. This assurance of God's providence and the conviction that He had work for me to do and would see me through until I had accomplished it remained with me all through my life.

Word came that Miss Frey was leaving on furlough and wished to see me before she went. Under cover of darkness, mother took me back to Ewha where I saw only Miss Frey and my doctor. After an examination of my sun-tanned body, the doctor said that I had baked away the terrible disease.

This was the last time I saw Miss Frey. She went on furlough and died the following year with cancer. Ewha College was started by her hand in 1910. She carried it on without the slightest doubt that Korean women, given an opportunity, in time would become educated leaders within their own country and would make contributions to the life of women all over the world. She kept her vision and worked the rest of her life to realize it.

In the meantime my two friends and several of the other imprisoned women were let out on bail. The Japanese government replaced the Military Governor with a civilian Governor-General who used "more lenient policies" in dealing with the Korean people. Schools were reopening in September.

Being well again, I wanted to return to my teaching post at Ewha. Others thought that I had better remain in hiding a while longer. Still disguised in old-fashioned dress and hairdo, I went to the village of Tang-woo-ri in Jaw-ju County to help in the educational program of the church. In the mornings we had the church kindergarten, and regular school classes in the afternoons for the younger girls. The program was strenuous but it was good to be doing something after so many months of idleness. The beauty and richness of country life during harvest season made a lasting impression upon my memory.

When the cold weather began in December, neither the kindergarten nor the girls' classes could be continued for lack of heat. I was tired and needed rest, so back to Seoul and home was a welcome release.

Early in January I returned to Ewha, for everyone agreed that conditions were more normal in Korea and that it would be safe for me to come out of hiding. The work program and the general situation at Ewha remained the same, but we were not the same persons. We were no longer docile and helpless people who accepted passively the injustices done to us. We sought indirect ways of expressing our patriotism. We did the ordinary work with a new motive. We would do everything well which would in the long run help us gain independence. Life and work took on a new meaning. In the summer of 1920, we heard that in India the great man of "soul force," Mahatma Gandhi, was leading the populace in a nationwide movement of nonviolence and noncooperation with British rule. The masses in both Korea and India had broken out against alien injustice and for their rights to personal liberty and national freedom.

We had to do something to express our devotion to the country. Direct actions for our national independence would get us nowhere. While within the country the movement was being trampled down by the iron heel of Japanese militarism, our repeated appeals to the international leaders and organizations of that time found no sympathetic response. Our problem was considered by them as solely a domestic concern of Japan. This indifference of the outside world to our independence movement was something we could hardly understand. Our assumption that the declarations of President Wilson would be applied and implemented in all international relations was all wrong, and because of this we felt discouraged and forsaken when the news reached us that our representative was denied attendance at the Paris Conference. However, we were determined to pursue the road toward independence until we achieved it. We were fully aware that our course of action included no violence and that we were doing wrong to no one. We were simply asserting our own rights.

Except for a few leaders who went into exile in other countries, we all remained within the country. Already the civic leaders were getting ready to organize Sin-kan-hoi, a new association for the betterment of our society. It had to be nonpolitical and only social in character, but all the leaders had the secret motive of turning it into political use whenever the opportunity afforded itself. Women's groups within and without the churches were feeling their way toward finding something to do for their country.

Infused with this deep-seated patriotism and renewed zeal, we finished the winter and spring terms at Ewha. Full three months of summer vacation were near at hand. We got busy planning how best to put this time to use. An idea came. The Korean people were mostly nonreligious, with only a few Christians among them. We at Ewha were devout Christians, with a certain sense of mission. Legally we had religious freedom and could hold services without restrictions. The idea was to form an Ewha evangelistic band and tour the country, preaching everywhere we went. Seven members composed the team: Esther Hong, Pauline Kim, Hannah

Kim, Sungduk Youn, Sindo Kim, Aieun Kim, and myself.

We could all sing and preach, or give our own testimony. Our talks had individual and social appeal, usually ending up with a highly patriotic note, for the ideals of human dignity and social justice are so linked with Christian teaching and practice that they are inseparable. "Christ died for us. We too must be willing to live or to die for our people if necessary. The welfare of the people, their health and education, their economic and social betterment should be our supreme concern." Such was the gist of the message.

Everywhere we went the churches were crowded and the meetings had to be held outdoors. Response from the people was beyond our dreams. In Sunchun, before the evening meeting was over more than five hundred raised their hands to show determination to follow Christ and serve their countrymen. This continued in town after town. But before we reached the last town on our first northwest trip between Seoul and Eui-ju, Japanese police began to take notice. They started to attend every meeting we held and to make notes on our speeches, interrupting quite often by saying, "Stop, that's an improper thing to say."

When we reached An-ju we met with strong resistance. Before I was half through speaking, the police stopped me altogether and took me to their police station. With a whip on the table between us, the police chief began to question me. After the usual questions and answers he struck the table with all his might and raised his voice. I knew he was trying to scare me out of my wits; but all the time, I was praying for the right words to say.

He shouted a question at me, "Why do you try to

instigate the people to another independence uprising?"
He was trying to trap me into a made-up case through
my own words.

My straight answer was, "I do no such thing. You
misinterpret my speeches. I am simply telling the people to believe in Christ and become good Christians."

Whipping the table he shouted again, "No, you lie.
You are telling them to live or die for Korean independence."

"No," I said calmly, "what I meant was to live or die
for the welfare of the people and for the betterment of
society. That's plain good citizenship. Don't you want
us to become good citizens?"

After an hour's heckling, he told me we could hold
no more meetings at An-ju or anywhere else. When I
tried to remind him that the law granted religious liberty, he refused to let me speak further and demanded
that I obey his order. He struck the table again and left
the room.

Thus the poor table got an extra whipping in my
place and our enthusiastic tour came to a sad end at
the close of the second week. Our original plan had been
to take two weeks each for the northwest, northeast,
southwest, and southeast tours, covering the entire
peninsula.

Early in 1921 our missionary teachers had suggested
that I go to the United States for further study. From
the beginning it had been their policy to train Koreans
for positions of leadership and I was to be given three
years abroad. However, Miss Jeannette Walter, our
interim president, felt the shortage of staff very keenly
and asked me if I would be willing to delay my departure one year.

After the sudden death of Miss Frey, there was a

vacuum of two years in our presidency and Miss Walter was filling it magnificently. She had helped me and nursed me through my early illness and of course that fact alone was enough to inspire me. With no hesitation my answer was in the affirmative. Also, whether I went abroad or not, whether the trip was delayed one year or more, these were all secondary matters to my way of thinking. The welfare of Ewha was the important consideration.

As a matter of fact, this year proved to be one of the most productive of my life. Working under Miss Walter and with my colleagues was a very happy and satisfying experience. The students and their problems became my vital concern in ever increasing measure. With some of the other Korean teachers, I lived in the dormitory with the students. This gave me the privilege of sharing life intimately with them. It was during this year that my place on the Ewha faculty became firmly established. The delay also made possible my trip to Peking and my part in planning the conference that led to the organization of the YWCA of Korea. I felt that God was in the delay.

It was in May, 1922, that Mrs. Pilly Kim Choi and I attended the Student Christian Federation Conference in Peking. We went with the YMCA delegation since as yet there was no Christian women's organization and we could therefore represent none. But as prospects for leadership, we were chosen to go and attend an international gathering, the first time for a woman in Korean history. The long train ride and contact with a strange environment, as well as first associations with so many worldwide personages, were highly stimulating and enriching experiences. Mrs. Choi and I were busy taking it all in, and our minds and hearts were ceaselessly planning how we could start a YWCA in Korea and link it up with the worldwide fellowship.

We talked with some of the delegates from the United States about our great desire for a YWCA organization. We learned that neither the World YWCA Committee nor the United States Foreign Division could come into Korea to help organize a YWCA without the permission of the Japanese organization. In other words, no nation of a colonial status could be visited by any national or international YWCA body without the consent of the YWCA of the colonial power. If we were to have a YWCA in Korea, we would have to start it ourselves. We could not and would not wait for outside help. Mrs. Choi and I returned home feeling that we must fulfill that responsibility since we were the first two Korean women to attend such a conference.

We lost no time. Mrs. Choi talked among the Presbyterian leaders and I the Methodist. Everyone we talked to was enthusiastic. So we planned an initiation conference to be held in early July.

Our women responded as though they had been waiting for such a call. They too had been groping for ways and means to release their pent-up patriotism and to follow up the awakening of the people in general, and of women in particular, with some concrete measures. A large representation of church women, Christian schoolteachers, and students came together. They carried on a full summer conference program, the first of its kind in Korea for women, with extra sessions to discuss plans to organize the YWCA. Such were the beginnings of the YWCA in Korea.

IV

AMERICAN UNIVERSITY LIFE

It was late in July, 1922, that I set out on my first trip across the Pacific. How thrilled I was. Miss Laura Edwards, an evangelistic missionary to Korea, was my traveling companion. We boarded the SS *President Wilson* at Yokohama. Everybody had given me advice on what to do if I got seasick! But from beginning to end the trip was full of wonder. Such a huge ship with all the conveniences of a hotel! I could hardly believe my eyes! Such comfort and luxury were way beyond my life at home and in the Ewha dormitory! Why should anyone get sick, I thought.

However, the food was so different from the Korean that I did not feel hungry sometimes. The basic difference between Western food and ours lies in the seasoning. In the main we use the same ingredients. But when we cook, soy sauce is used in place of salt, and sesame oil instead of butter or other cooking oil. And we add red pepper powder, toasted sesame seed powder, and chopped green onions and garlic. Our soups, stews, cooked vegetables, or salads taste totally different from Western food, which in general is very bland to us. No matter how much we eat of the Western food, we still feel hungry for ours.

Our distinctive national dish, *kimchee,* is made up of raw vegetables well fermented and blended into one glorious taste nowhere else to be found except in Korea. When we make *kimchee* late in the fall for winter use, it is just like canning time in an American farm home. At this particular season, the streets in all directions are a maze of stalls, heaped high with vegetables in preparation for *kimchee* making. Everybody in the family stops other work and helps salt down the long cabbages, wash them in the ice-cold water, and fill up between the leaves with mixed seasonings—red pepper, long onions, ginger, garlic, chestnuts, apples, and pears. At Ewha we used to recess school a few days for *kimchee* making, and called it *kimchee* vacation. For this and other dishes I began to feel hungry from the second day on shipboard.

Every evening there was some entertainment, a movie, music, or dancing. On the last evening after the Captain's dinner there was to be a dress parade. All the passengers were supposed to wear funny, beautiful, or unusual costumes.

I was carrying with me a traditionally formal Korean dress, the kind that a woman wears only once or twice in her lifetime—at her wedding or at the sixtieth birthday celebration, if she lives that long. I put on this dress with all its paraphernalia. It was a colorful, distinctive, and handsome costume. The *chima* was bright red, the *cho-gori* bright yellow, and over these was a coat of green silk with multi-colored striped sleeves. A red band of rich embroidery was used as a sash with a long flowing bow tied to the back. The crown was of black silk adorned with bright-colored jewels which shimmered and sparkled under the glittering lights. Everyone liked it and all through the dinner I could hear comments on how beautiful it was. Of course this made me feel proud of my dress and my country. After dinner we all lined up and paraded in front of the judges. To my happy surprise my dress was given the first prize for being the most beautiful one.

After nine days at sea, we landed at Seattle, Washington. At Denver, Colorado, Miss Edwards and I separated, for she went South while I was going to Wichita, Kansas. All during the voyage she had been a wonderful companion, telling me what to expect and how to meet new circumstances. Besides, she was a part of home still lingering with me. When this last touch of home was gone, I felt painfully lonesome and homesick. Tears flowed all night in the Pullman car.

New hope and joy revived when in Wichita the families and friends of Miss Walter, Miss Morris, and Miss Conrow met me at the station. Although it was the very first meeting, we felt we had known each other for a long time, so vivid had been Miss Walter's and Miss Morris' letters and descriptions.

I can never forget the first night spent with the Morris family. Luella Noble, the youngest sister, who lived with her father in their big stone house on River Boulevard, took me to their home. The great mansion with a spacious garden was lovely and the furniture arrangement and other interior decorations were so beautiful that I felt like Alice in Wonderland. There were so many different turns made during the tour of the house it was hard to tell where I was—in a palace, in a museum, or in a lovely home. But the guest bedroom upstairs was the greatest surprise. With a high ceiling and Gothic windows, it was more like a cathedral than a bedroom. I was led up to it and told to make myself at home. Although everything was in perfect order with a nice big bed and mahogany furniture, I felt so strange I could not go to sleep for a long while.

After a short stay in Wichita, visiting with different families, I went to Kingman, Kansas, to spend the summer with Miss Walter's parents. Miss Walter had made all the arrangements before I left home. Her plan was to orient me to American life and have her people in

Kingman and Wichita help me get ready to go to Ohio Wesleyan University, in Delaware, that fall. Kingman was a small, quiet town and the people were kind and friendly. I felt at home right away with Mr. and Mrs. Walter. They gave me a nice room upstairs. Their bedroom was also on this floor, but I felt quite alone the first few nights. Korean houses have all the rooms on one floor around a court with only sliding doors of one thin layer of paper, so you do not feel so separated although you are put into different rooms. But here, when I went upstairs into my bedroom and closed the door, I was all alone.

There was a back yard with a small garden and chicken house. Mrs. Walter fried a chicken every Sunday. She did all the housework by herself. I tried to help some, but never was good. Life became quite normal for me in about a week.

Then all of a sudden I began to feel very sick. The Kansas summer heat became unbearable and my whole body weighted me down with aches. Finally the family doctor was called. After a few days' examinations and tests he declared the sickness to be typhoid fever. Up to that time nobody had ever thought that one going to the United States needed precautionary inoculations. Judging by the time I developed the fever the doctor said I must have picked up the germ on the ship. He told me that I would get good care at the Methodist hospital in Wichita. But the Walters said I could either go to the hospital or stay with them under Dr. Potter's care. "You decide what you want to do," they said. I was too sick and lonesome to think about the inconveniences I would cause the Walters if I stayed. My instant answer was, "I want to be sick at home."

So they turned their parlor into a temporary hospital

room, for upstairs was too hot in the afternoons. They had to keep all their friends and their grandchildren away. Doctor Potter, a trained nurse, and her assistant took good professional care of me night and day; and Mr. and Mrs. Walter watched and loved me all the time. Father and Mother Walter were twentieth-century Good Samaritans. They even paid all my bills, which I knew only vaguely were very high.

Not until the middle of October was I able to go to Ohio Wesleyan University. Delaware is a college town near Columbus, and there again I felt at home and liked everything from the beginning. Classic-looking college buildings connected by streets lined with rows of old trees, and beautiful lawns and woods at every turn made me feel as though I were in a fairyland. And Grey Chapel towered over the small college town reminding everyone that culture of the mind and spirit is to be sought after rather than gold. I liked the town, the campus, and every building on it.

Fortunately I was assigned to live in the oldest women's dormitory, Monnett Hall. It was a building full of traditions, and juniors and seniors had priority in living there. Esther Beck, who had studied at Ewha and had been a friend for a long time, was already there to welcome me. Her parents were early missionaries in Korea and Esther had grown up going to schools in Korea. She went to the English-speaking schools with other foreign children in the lower grades, but came to Ewha for her high school work.

We were roommates the first year in Monnett and she helped me to get adjusted to the strange, new campus life. She and I had a great deal in common besides our Korean background. She was a student volunteer getting ready to go back to Korea as a second-generation missionary. She was talented in music, while I had a great appreciation of it. We took several courses together in Bible and English literature. It meant so much to have the fellowship and guidance of such a congenial friend during the first year in a new country.

The work I had done at Ewha College was given credit in the registrar's office for two years at Ohio Wesleyan. So I could register for the junior year, with the exception of the course in English. In no uncertain terms I was told that I must take the freshman English course, as all foreign students were required to do. Going over the outline of the freshman course, I found that much of its content was what I had already studied at Ewha College. I protested that although I was a foreign student, I would like to make my own choice; that if the junior English was too difficult, I could at least manage the sophomore course. The registrar answered that no foreign student at the university had ever started with the sophomore course. He kept his stand and I kept mine. At last he said that permission would be granted if I submitted a satisfactory composition and brought it to him the next day on the subject "Why I Do Not Want the Freshman English Course."

This gave me the chance to explain that I had looked through the text outline and found the material had already been covered at Ewha and that I had not come so far merely to repeat what I had studied before. "I left urgent work at home," I wrote. "Every minute is precious and must count for some gain in knowledge or in experience. I object to taking the freshman English since it would be a pure waste of time." Two days later the registrar reported that the English teachers had read my composition and were willing for me to take the sophomore course.

As professors unlocked new doors into the treasure-house of human experience, I felt enchanted and at times almost swept off my feet. It made me want to pursue further studies into many fields such as religion, philosophy, and English literature. Not only the subject matter, but the personalities of the professors made a great impression on me. Professor Rollin H. Walker was an eminent biblical scholar as well as one of the best loved of the professors. Oftentimes we could not tell whether we were learning him or his course. Dr. Trumbell Gillett Duvall taught us how to think effectively as he gave the content of his courses. Students in general did not seem to care for philosophy, but studying with him we loved it—so much so that for awhile I thought I would like to major in this field. Dean William Emory Smyser's courses on Tennyson and Browning almost made them come to life again in our midst. And so it went. The broadening and deepening effects of the university curriculum and its professors were beyond my expectations.

When I arrived at Ohio Wesleyan there were three Korean men students enrolled—Kihoo Kim, Do-yun Kim, and Hyung-ki Lew. We had very little to do with each other except when we got together to cook and eat some Korean dishes at the home where Mr. Lew was boarding. All of us carried over to this American university campus our traditional upbringing of not having anything to do with the opposite sex. Of the three, only Mr. Lew was a Christian and this meant a common interest between us at a deep level. Both of us were in Dr. Walker's Bible class and in Professor John Tryon Marshman's speech course, but we never talked or sat together. However, before the year was over he and I became good friends, the first man friend I had ever had with whom I could talk and share experiences. He graduated at the end of the year and went to Garrett Biblical Institute in Evanston. There he met and fell in love with Julia Syn, the only member of our fourth graduating class of Ewha College. They returned to Korea to serve in the Korean Methodist Church. Mr. Lew became Secretary for Christian Education of the General Board of the church. Years afterward he became a bishop and served for two terms. He is an eminent scholar in the field of biblical studies and at the present time is compiling and editing a dictionary of the Bible.

All four of the Korean students at Wesleyan had to work part time. I had a full scholarship to pay for all the major expenses, but I needed some pin money and I wanted to take private voice lessons. I was fortunate enough to get a library job in the evenings. I could sit at the desk and study when I was not answering questions or attending to requests for books.

Once the student employment bureau called and asked me to baby-sit. I accepted without any idea of what it was going to be like. When as a disguised *amah* I had helped to take care of the children in whose home I stayed while I was hiding after the independence uprising, the mother was always in the house. This time both the parents were gone, and two small children and a baby were left entirely in my care. The evening was long and I perspired, not so much with heavy work as with the terrifying sense of responsibility and of my inadequacy to cope with the situation. The next day I went to the student employment office and said, "Please, no more baby-sitting for me!"

What to do and where to be during the three-months-long summer vacation was a real problem and had to be faced. Early in May I received an invitation to spend the summer with my friend and former teacher at Ewha, Miss Marsook Syn. She was one of the three graduates of our famous first class of 1914. She had come to America in 1919 and had established a small rooming house of her own in Philadelphia. She said I could come and help with the housework and we could get our own meals together at a very small expense, which she could easily manage. I accepted the offer and went to her.

We had fun together cooking Korean dishes and thinking and talking about home and friends back in Korea. Besides keeping the rooming house, she was doing all kinds of odd jobs to make sure of extra income. She inspired me to look for a job too, for there was a great deal of time on my hands after the housework was finished. So with a newspaper advertisement in hand, she and I went up and down the streets of Philadelphia calling on possible employers. Rejections one after another for three days were really discouraging. At the end of the third day my friend said, "I told you it wouldn't be possible to find a summer job in Philadelphia. Just rest your mind and take it easy with me. You had a hard year at the college and need a rest." She was very comforting and reassuring in her friendship and willingness to support me all summer.

The next morning I found in the paper an advertisement for some work in a laundry. When I asked my friend to go with me to apply for this work she exclaimed, "Oh no, you cannot work in the steaming heat of a laundry." But I insisted and we went. Right away the proprietor said I could begin work the next morning. I was almost hilarious over getting the job, but my friend was dubious. Anyway, against her protests I went to the laundry the next day. My work was to shake out wet sheets and pillow cases and feed them

61

into the electric ironer. The shaking out process was hard work; my breath was short, my arms ached. The physical labor was beyond my strength and before the week was up I was sick. My friend did not need to tell me I had to stop.

By the time I went back to school in the fall, my health was in good shape again. The second year at Ohio Wesleyan ran along much more smoothly than the first in all my academic subjects. The poorest grade I ever made was in political science—the study of American government. This experience made me fight shy the rest of my life at anything that is prefixed by the adjective "political," although in the course of events I was to become involuntarily involved in the concerns of my own government.

Realizing it to be my last year at the university and with better health and better choice of courses, I concentrated a great deal upon my studies. The two years of my life at Ohio Wesleyan were literally consecrated at the altar of academic pursuits. "There is so much to learn and two years are too short a time to waste any of it on other things." This had been my stubborn stand.

Usually on Friday and Saturday evenings many girls from the dormitory went out on dates. For me, both from the point of view of time and of our traditional Korean way of thinking, dates were taboo from the beginning. At first I did not know what the word *date* meant, but soon I learned from Esther who would go out on dates when Olin Stockwell came to see her. Olin had graduated from Ohio Wesleyan the year before and was studying theology at Garrett Biblical Institute. They were engaged to be married after Esther graduated and were to go back to Korea as missionaries. To our disappointment, however, they were sent to China instead.

In 1950 Olin was imprisoned by the Chinese Communists and remained in prison for two years. He is now president of Trinity Theological College in Singapore.

In the fall of 1923 I had the opportunity to attend the Executive Committee Meeting of the Woman's Foreign Missionary Society of the Methodist Episcopal Church. The scope of this meeting was nationwide. It was a wonderful revelation to see hundreds of churchwomen come together to pray and work for their common objectives and responsibilities concerning missions in all parts of the world.

I was deeply impressed by Mrs. Thomas Nicholson, who was the national president. The way she conducted the meetings and managed everything impressed me so much that I enjoyed sitting in the group watching her. Her hold on me was so strong that I got up the courage to ask her for a personal interview when she could give it. At the end of one of the sessions, she beckoned me to meet her behind the stage. I took out a piece of paper on which I had typewritten a plan to organize all the women of the world for fellowship and Christian action. She said she would take the sheet of paper "as a challenge," and in later years she attributed to me the original idea that led to the establishing of the World Association of Methodist Women. There is nothing unusual about this idea except that it came to me as early as it did.

Mrs. Nicholson has been a constant inspiration to me since I saw her for the first time in 1923. Her friendship, sympathy, understanding, and love have been continued all through the years, and she has been one of the strongest supporters of our Ewha Womans University.

My part on the program was to make a speech on the

needs of Ewha. At the same time I was to make a presentation to the Society of the old Ewha bell, which was in turn to be presented to the historical museum of the missionary society in Boston. It was a good Korean brass bell with a forceful tone. I knew this, for it was the bell I had rung for over five years. Korean bells are famous for their rich, ringing tones.

So with the bell in hand I was ready to make a speech in the evening, after which I was to take the midnight train back to Delaware for an examination the next morning. To my keen disappointment my talk was crowded out and was postponed until the next session. I hardly knew what to do. I quickly wrote down the speech I had intended to make and gave it to Miss Walter to present for me when the time came. The central thought of the speech was an appeal for twenty-five thousand dollars to buy the Sinchon campus on which to build and expand our growing Ewha College.

My mission for Ewha did not end in failure, though I did not know until later what happened ten thousand miles away, in Seoul, on that very day! We had no air mail in those days, but in due time Mrs. Nicholson received a letter from Dr. Alice Appenzeller reporting what happened on the day I was to speak at Des Moines. Let her tell the story:

The day was rainy. Our spirits were low. There were visitors, Mrs. Phillips Gray, her daughter, and a friend from Detroit. I took them around and made the best showing I could of our quarters, and then Mrs. Gray said, "Have you any special needs?" I had not mentioned them for I was waiting for guidance. I clenched my hands behind my back and prayed, "O God, help me to tell her!"

I told her how difficult it was to buy land, of the available site, and how we must buy it at once or lose the chance. Quietly but with my heart pounding I said,

"Would you like to see this wonderful place for a campus?"

She would; so I called an old taxi and we went out in the country to see the site, which has been called one of the most ideal in the world. The ladies saw the possibilities, and when we returned Mrs. Gray asked if I would excuse her and her daughter for a few minutes. They cabled to their Detroit banker to send $35,000 to Ewha College, Seoul, Korea.

So the bank forwarded the funds and God was able to accomplish His purpose, having found spirits sensitive to His guidance. Thus was demonstrated the power of united prayer regardless of geography, boundaries, seas, and outer space.

Thus the "modern miracle" of Ewha began to take place in the northwest corner of Seoul among the pine-wooded hills.

Before I realized it, graduation was taking place. In June, 1924, I received the bachelor of arts degree. I had worked hard on my studies because I enjoyed them and because I felt a heavy responsibility for learning all I could during these years away from Korea. I had not known until commencement that there was such a society as Phi Beta Kappa. Friends told me it was an honorary society for people with the highest quality of scholarship. I was awarded membership in it, but at that time I did not know enough to appreciate its value.

Following commencement, it was my privilege to go to Washington, D.C., to attend the World Committee Meeting of the YWCA. After the conference of 1922 in Peking, the Korean YWCA had been able to organize several city and student groups. Then the representatives had come together and organized their own National Committee. This Committee in Korea asked me to attend the World Committee and request our affiliation with the world fellowship. This was a responsibility greatly welcomed and enthusiastically discharged by me. It was also the first international gathering I attended in the United States. Some of the lasting friendships of my life were started at this time.

But here again there were difficulties in the way of obtaining membership because we were too young and untried and unknown as an organization. Through all YWCA history, in no other country had the women of the land taken the entire initiative and responsibility for the beginning of their organization. After much discussion we were granted "pioneer membership." This was the status usually given to groups in the embryo stage. No one in Korea knew exactly what this membership meant, but we were satisfied with any kind of recognition. Linking up with a world organization in any fashion was enough cause for rejoicing.

After this meeting I went to New York and enrolled in the summer session of the YWCA training school. My interest in the YWCA made me feel the need of getting all the help I could. Six weeks of concentrated training gave me substantial preparation to serve for many years as a volunteer in the development of the Korean YWCA.

While I was in New York, a conference of the Korean Student Association took place. There I met many men for the first time. I had become much more liberal in the past two years, so had dates with several of them. One man, Mr. Hong, noticed that I did not have a watch. He was surprised and tried to give me one the next time he took me out. He presented it saying, "From a friend to a friend." I had to refuse, telling him, "I know you are merely thinking about my need as a good friend, but I cannot take it. This is the kind of behavior I am going to tell my students not to engage in when I return home. How could I accept your gift now and then later say to my students that such things are not proper etiquette?" He understood and put it back into his pocket saying, "You are right. I respect what you have done."

For my third school year in America, I went to Boston in September and registered in the philosophy department of the graduate school of Boston University. My interest in philosophy and religion was very keen by this time, so I took courses in these fields. My major professor was Dr. Edgar S. Brightman. He directed my thesis on "The Relation Between Philosophy and Religion." It was a rare privilege to be working under such brilliant and inspiring personalities as Professor Brightman, Professor Knudson, and Dean Athearn. Professor Brightman gave most generously of his time and energy to help me finish the work for the MA degree in one year. He urged me to stay on two more years and obtain a doctorate before returning home. When I wrote to Dr. Walker at Ohio Wesleyan for his advice on the matter, he wrote back, "The woods are thick with PhD's, but there is only one Helen Kim. Go back home to your work now as you planned. Life is long and this is not going to be your only chance." This settled the question happily for me.

In Boston I lived in Franklin Square House, a dormitory for women run at a very reasonable cost. In the same house was Miss Laura Yi, one of the teachers from Ewha who had come to Boston two years ahead of me. Later in the fall of 1924 Miss Mary E. Young, also a missionary teacher from Ewha, joined us. Miss Young had been my music teacher at Ewha and I had been inspired to emulate her unselfish spirit as I observed her life among us. We three had some good times together when we were not too much occupied by our studies.

I found also a new friend in Boston, Miss Ayoung Lim. She was studying full time at the Boston Conservatory of Music where I went every week for voice lessons. Once we had met, we became fast friends. We helped each other to overcome some of the inner struggles that are so intensely real to young people, but which disappear like vapor as time passes and are no longer recognizable as problems. Mutual understanding and sympathy kept us afloat until we safely landed on the other shore of maturer years.

In 1924, Boston University had no real campus. The buildings were scattered throughout the city. From Franklin Square House to Boylston Street and back, I had to walk through the Public Garden. The most beautiful season was in the spring when the tulips were blooming against the background of beautiful spring greenery. Pausing to enjoy the exquisite beauty, I often wondered whether another garden anywhere else would ever mean so much to me. Walking on the esplanade by the Charles river in the moonlight I wondered whether or not I could ever find a more romantic spot in all the world. I was always alone at these times. With me the loftiest heights of romance in nature are attainable only when alone. It must be the feeling akin to two close friends wanting to be by themselves.

As soon as the second semester closed early in June, before returning to Korea I packed up my bags and left Boston for the Korean Student Association meetings in Chicago. In Chicago I was asked to make a talk on my thesis for the MA degree. Afterward one of the outstanding leaders of the Association, Mr. Duk-soo Chang, wanted to discuss the thesis with me further. We talked for awhile. He told me something about his work in political science, then asked me whether we could be friends. He was a famous orator, an accomplished scholar, and an established leader in our society in general and in the independence movement in particular. Friendship with him would be a rare privilege and I accepted it gladly.

While I was in Delaware and in Boston, Sundays were devoted to church and its activities. Young people's groups and women's missionary societies on local and district levels often asked me to come and talk about Korea and the Korean church or to give my testimony as a Christian. I was always glad to do this, for it gave me precious contact with like-minded people. I was also able to observe how the church work was carried on in the United States.

So with all these varied experiences, in addition to two degrees and with very light luggage, I boarded the SS *President Cleveland* late in June 1925, homeward bound. Three years in the United States had made it my second home. I was sorry to leave all the professors and friends who had meant so much to me. On the other hand I was eager to get back and share my rich experiences with family, friends, and students. The days and hours on the steamer seemed unusually long.

V

HOME AGAIN

When the SS *President Cleveland* docked at Yokohama harbor in July 1925, my first welcome was by a member of the Japanese Intelligence. He asked me to go to the police station to be questioned. I asked, "Have I done something wrong?" He answered, "No, but we want to know what you did in America. We want to ask you many questions." "In that case you may ask the questions here and now," I said. "I have baggage to attend to and I must not miss the first train to Shimonoseki."

So he and I had a long session. He probed into my three years' stay, wanting to know what I studied, whom I met, and what I thought about America. I think he was relieved to find out that my academic subjects had not been in the field of political science and that I had not joined any of the political organizations of the Koreans in the United States.

Although I was the last one coming ashore, I was able to make all the expected connections and arrived on schedule in Seoul, where family and friends were anxiously looking for me. The joy of coming home was complete. The first words of my friends were, "You have not changed a bit. We expected to see you different." They were pleased and meant to say it as a compliment, but it worried me a little. "I hope the three years have done something to me inside even if it doesn't show on the outside," was my reply.

I went to the dormitory at Ewha and my parents remained with friends until we could find our own house.

They had gone to Peking to live with my sister Ellen and my brother John while I was away in the United States and had returned to Seoul just before my arrival. Within a week we found a small, thatched-roof house in Song-wol Dong suburb. This was a poor section of the city and the house was old, but it was all our own. Mother always said to me, "A filial son or daughter should never have old parents live in a house other than their own. You never know when they will die, and death in rented or borrowed quarters is a terrible thing." This idea and logic belong to the old traditions; for, though mother broke with many of the old customs, others stayed with her all her life. Father was always quiet, but fully endorsed mother's ideas and actions.

We had a fine time converting this house into our home, even adding a new room big enough to accommodate a desk for me. We were a very happy and proud family with a home near my work and close to our church. Father and mother became active participants in all its work, including the daily visitation of homes. But in a few months' time our family reunion was interrupted.

In addition to my teaching schedule, Dr. Alice Appenzeller, our new president, asked me to live in the dormitory. The matron was getting married and someone was needed to replace her. As much as I liked to be with the girls, I felt this to be too much of an added burden; but when the President went over the names of all the Korean teachers and pointed out that I was the only one of the "older girls" left to do it, I had no more argument. So back to the dormitory I went and lived with the girls for five more years.

Very soon after I went into the dormitory, I proposed to the girls that we organize ourselves for complete self-management. They liked the idea and set themselves to work at once. They organized their own committees according to regulations that they had drawn up and that had received faculty approval.

They made their own budget and collected their own fees. They planned their own menus and either did their own marketing or supervised their errand man as he did it. They employed cooks and other workers in the kitchen to do the heavy work while they were in classes, but it was all done under their direction and supervision. Any irregularities were dealt with by their own committee on discipline and only a few major cases were brought to my attention and to the faculty. The experiment was a thrilling success.

Of course, the responsibilities and working hours were heavy at times for the girls, but they all liked the arrangement. Students of those days had no outside interests or attractions. Life within the college was all they had, so the extra work did not mean any sacrifice on their part. On the other hand, it gave them an unprecedented opportunity to develop their sense of responsibility and leadership qualities. The graduates of this period always demonstrated greater initiative and leadership in their private and public life than the groups of other years. It was a genuine piece of democratic education.

From the time that Miss Appenzeller took over the presidency, which was in the early years of the twenties, she wanted to get the Christian denominations that were working in Korea to participate in a joint support of the College. I remember her happiness when in 1925 the Southern Methodist missions began their cooperation with the Methodist Episcopal missions in Korea, giving to the College an annual subsidy and also sending us a missionary faculty member. The new status helped to strengthen the departments of literature and music, and the graduates of these departments were given licenses to teach in private girls' high schools.

In 1929 the United Church of Canada missions joined in the cooperative support of Ewha and made possible the establishment, with government permit, of a new Department of Home Economics, the first of its kind in Korea. It soon outgrew the older departments in size. The Presbyterian Church has always contributed fine faculty members in the field of Christian Education as well as teachers for the English Department. So from its early days our college became an ecumenical concern.

I had a full schedule of teaching in the two fields of English and Christian Education. I was given also the responsibility of directing the entire curriculum in the latter field. This was a very important task and Miss Appenzeller convinced me that the success or failure of our entire enterprise depended upon this phase of our program. It meant a reevaluation and reorganization of the religious education courses for all four years of the college curriculum. During the first two years the students were to study the Bible; in the last two years they were to increase their knowledge of and preparation for the practical application of Christian teachings to life. I had to teach many of the new courses until some help came. It was a very exciting job. Some of the keenest minds of the students were stimulated, and bright flashes went back and forth among us as we discussed basic issues that touched upon our lives. Our emotions were stirred as we faced together the revelation of inconsistencies between Christian principles and actual practice in history as well as in our current society.

Just before I returned from America, Ewha College

had gone through reorganization according to the current Japanese regulations and had become a government-recognized special school. In 1926, at the beginning of the new academic year, President Appenzeller asked me to become the dean of the college. "We have been waiting for a Korean leader. With your vision and zeal for a woman's college in Korea, and with your academic preparation and practical experience we need you." She gave me no chance to think or to say no. I was very inadequately prepared for administration, but she wanted a Korean to take the position. I couldn't refuse her, so accepted it, hoping I would be adequate to meet its requirements.

The only actual difference evident in taking this new responsibility was moving into a small but private office across the hall from the President's. The attitude of my faculty colleagues remained the same. We were just a large family of like-minded people. The missionaries and Koreans worked side by side. Some had been my teachers. One of the old Korean teachers who had taught me Chinese classics was Mr. Keuk-pac Kim. He said, "I don't feel any different toward you from the way I have always felt. You were a good student and I hope you continue to be one." Such was our relationship as fellow workers. A private office only facilitated and strengthened the ties.

There was someone else who took advantage of this small but private office. Early one morning the gateman came and told me I had a caller. When I went down to the office, my father was sitting calmly on a chair. I thought maybe something had happened at home and asked, "What is it, father?" He answered, "Nothing in particular. I wanted to see you." After that I knew what to expect when I was told that I had an early caller.

Mother was busy in her church activities, but father had to come to see me sometimes. Students also found it convenient to come to the private room for all kinds of problems.

Our faculty organized a research association to encourage each other to continue in special studies. We started with bimonthly meetings at which different members made reports on the progress of their work. We soon realized that these meetings were meaningless. There was a great variety of subject matter but there were not enough people in any one field to understand and evaluate the reports. So we discontinued the meetings and tried to establish channels for academic fellowship with the faculties of other colleges. Under the prevailing systems and practices, these attempts were also unfruitful. We felt as though our own academic life was stifled and longed for some new breath of air. However, on the whole, we as individuals and the college we were serving were growing along together very markedly.

Miss Appenzeller believed that the liberation of mind and spirit should not be curtailed by customs and traditions, or limited to narrow loyalties and allegiances. She led us to a broader view of what a Christian woman can be. She had what we now call an ecumenical mind. When we were trying to organize our own YWCA in Korea, she was always behind us and encouraged us to break down denominational barriers and become ecumenical in our outlook and in our efforts to better the conditions of the life of women in Korea.

My life in the College was full and happy. Being in the dormitory, I was on duty practically twenty-four hours a day. But it never bothered me, for none of us lived under the pressure of time in those days and we never knew the difference between long and short working days. My Sundays were full too, for from my early childhood I was accustomed to a full Sunday program. Chung Dong church had been our family church since we moved to Seoul, so whatever this church wanted me to do I accepted as my Christian responsibility.

Soon after I returned from America, I was asked to teach a young people's class and take charge of the Youth Department of the Sunday school. At the same time I was put on the Board of Stewards and on the Epworth League committee. Often I was elected to the District and Annual Conferences of the Methodist Church. My responsibilities as a churchwoman grew by leaps and bounds. In 1928 I was elected a lay delegate to the General Conference of the Methodist Episcopal Church held in Kansas City, Missouri. But I could not have gone abroad again had it not been for the generous grant of leave of absence from Ewha College. Both the President and my colleagues felt the importance of such meetings and made it possible for me to be away.

During the General Conference, an alarming situation developed. We reached a deadlock in our election of the last one of the bishops. Ballot after ballot brought no results. So the Conference stopped balloting to discuss how to meet the situation. After all kinds of arguments, the consensus of the Conference was toward the abolishment of an episcopal area so that further election of a bishop would not be necessary. The concrete measure suggested was to merge the Philippines and Korea into a single area instead of continuing them as two separate ones, each with its own resident bishop. I could not remain quiet; and against the advice of my fellow delegates from Korea, Dr. Hugh Heung-wu Cynn and Rev. Sung-ok Pynn, who thought it was no use for me to protest the plan, I asked for the floor.

76

Bishop Herbert Welch, who was presiding at the session, recognized me and asked me to come up to the platform and speak through the microphone. My heart was pounding because of the shock of the suggested loss of our bishop and the excitement of having to make a speech. I do not remember the exact words, but the main point of my faltering speech was, "If two areas have to be merged, why not select two areas where the distance is much less than between Korea and the Philippines? (There were no jet flights in 1928.) Moreover, in Korea our church and its related institutions have grown tremendously in recent years under Bishop Welch, our first resident bishop. Both the church and the institutions are at the very strategic stage where constant direction and attention need to be given by the bishop. We need a whole bishop and not half of one. I am sure that it is not God's will for the General Conference to do this."

As I was closing my simple plea the whole Conference rose up, some applauding and some in tears, for the Holy Spirit worked in our midst, warmed our hearts, and turned the tide toward God. The Conference decided to continue balloting. On the first ballot Dr. E. Stanley Jones was elected and there was a great ovation for him and for the accomplishment of electing another bishop. The next morning Dr. Jones resigned, but Bishop James Baker was elected and Korea had a whole bishop.

All this made us appreciate in a special way Bishop Baker's service to our church. He was with us as our resident bishop until the autonomous Korean Methodist Church was organized in 1930 and the relationship with the Methodist Church in the United States changed from an organic to a fraternal one.

Among the liaison bishops to Korea was Bishop
Richard C. Raines, who made several trips to Korea and
came to Ewha when we were occupying tents and shacks
on our refugee campus in Pusan. Bishop Hazen G.
Werner came just after we had moved back to Seoul,
when the university was destitute. From that time he
showed a vital interest in our work and has been our
constant friend and helper.

My responsibilities in the YWCA and in the Student
Christian Movement continued. These organizations
had no means to afford regularly employed staff members. Everything had to be done by volunteers. Many of
my late afternoons and evenings were devoted to this
work, as well as most of my vacation days in winter and
summer. Even for a minimum program there were always desk work, personal interviews, meetings, and
conferences to be planned and implemented. The National Committee of the YWCA was composed of a
group of faithful women who felt the YWCA was their
very own. It was a joy to work with women who poured
their love, their time, and their meager possessions
into the foundation of this organization.

During those first years of our YWCA, our office was
in the YMCA building where space was graciously
loaned to us by our brethren. As time passed, we felt
the need of our own headquarters. Mrs. Eun-kyung
Hong of the National Committee found a small Korean
house for sale on the main street of Seoul. Although
the house was old and small it was adequate for the
program of that time. The location was better than we
could have wished for, so the Committee decided to buy
it and we pooled our resources. But even such a small
place was beyond our purchasing power. Fully aware of
the risk, we borrowed one thousand dollars and bought

the property. Then we wrote to Miss Sarah Lyon, the Executive Secretary for the Foreign Division of the YWCA of the United States and requested help to the extent of one thousand dolars. After some correspondence, this first monetary grant from our outside fellowship came. Our Committee members felt very grateful and we were relieved of our anxiety. Even to this day those who shared this experience talk about it with satisfaction and gratitude. This building was a stepping-stone toward the purchase of the present quarters.

In the summer of 1925 the first conference of the Institute of Pacific Relations took place in Honolulu, and a Korean delegation participated as a charter member. In 1927 the second conference was called again in Honolulu. On account of the expense, only a small delegation of three members was sent from Korea. My age and experience did not warrant such an honor, but because I was able to handle the English language I was asked to join Mr. Uk-kyum Yu and Mr. Kwan-soo Paik, and act as spokesman for the group. My colleagues at the College were enthusiastic and even helped to raise part of my travel expenses. Not only this time, but every time I was requested to go abroad and attend some international gathering, they accepted extra responsibilities in order to make it possible for me to go.

And so I went to Honolulu and attended the second conference of the Institute of Pacific Relations. Already the Institute members from different countries showed greater concern over the economic and political situations around the Pacific than for the cultural and racial, as in the beginning. Consequently the presence of a Korean delegation became a thorn in the flesh to the Japanese.

When our turn came for a statement, the whole point

of my speech was a plea for the preservation and encouragement of the cultural and racial identity of the Korean people along with others over whom aliens of stronger nations were ruling. We could not mention our desire for political independence and then return home in safety, so that was purposely avoided. But the conference seemed to understand the implications. Great personalities like Mrs. Carrie Chapman Catt and Professor William H. Kilpatrick were there. Mrs. Catt afterward compared my speech to that of Portia and called me "Portia" in a joking way at informal times. Dr. Kilpatrick later became my professor and counselor at Columbia, always encouraging and inspiring me to greater efforts for my people and my country.

Back at home I had to pay a heavy price for the innocent speech made in Honolulu and for contacting Dr. Syngman Rhee, the man whom the Japanese government hated the most. Our delegation felt we must call on him as our leader, although he had nothing to do with the Institute. We were glad to see each other and we exchanged views on our situations both within and outside the country. This was my very first personal encounter with Dr. Rhee. His patriotism and devotion to our independence movement were evident in all his thoughts and actions as we talked. I came away greatly impressed by his personality and with ever increasing respect for his undertakings in the cause of our independence.

There had been no special political significance in our meeting, but the mere fact of our contact with him was objectionable to the Japanese officials. I do not remember how many times I was called to the police headquarters and asked to account for all the things which had happened in Honolulu. My name must have gone on their blacklist this time, if not before.

In Seoul a formless group-solidarity was being felt among the leaders of the society. The YMCA at that time served as the focal point of all the Christian national leaders. It was through the YMCA and its General Secretary that the contacts were established with the Institute of Pacific Relations. To this group of leaders were added Mr. Sung-soo Kim, the founder and president of Posung College; Mr. Chin-wu Song and Mr. Kwan-soo Paik of *Dong-A* daily newspaper; the Reverend Joo-sam Ryang, an eminent leader of Protestantism; Mr. Uk-kyum Yu of the Union Christian College for Men; and myself from Ewha, the Christian college for women. We had no formal organization but we got together at the call of anyone and discussed whatever problems were presented. People from within the country as well as from without called on us as individuals or as a group to make contacts for educational, cultural, economic or other considerations. This unorganized group became an unofficial nucleus for influencing the affairs of our country.

When the third conference of the Institute of Pacific Relations was held in Kyoto, Japan, in 1929, I joined the delegation again. From the beginning the atmosphere was hostile to our group and we suspected something would happen. The Secretary General of the Institute begged for our understanding and asked us to leave quietly. "We are very sorry," he said, "but when the issue is put up to the Institute to choose between Korean participation or Japanese, we really have no alternative." So the Korean delegation, one of the charter members of the Institute, got "kicked out through the back door," for we were not even allowed to say good-bye.

We packed up and left Kyoto with a very bad taste in our mouths.

Strangely enough, after our liberation from the Japanese at the end of World War II, when we tried to renew contacts with the Institute of Pacific Relations, our repeated attempts were of no avail. At last we were told that we cannot return until Korea is united. We cannot help but suspect that there must be other elements besides prewar Japanese hostility which still keep us out.

Because of my church connections I was asked to attend the International Missionary Council to be held in Jerusalem in April, 1928. Prior to this conference I attended the meeting of the Far East Christian Leaders in Shanghai in early January. From Shanghai I boarded the SS *Ile de France* with two travel companions, Dr. Heung-wu Cynn, who was a fellow delegate to Jerusalem, and Mr. Pyung-sun Hong, YMCA rural secretary. We traveled together from Shanghai to France, through Europe, and on to Jerusalem. It was the first trip through Europe for all three of us, and we were busy gaining new experiences individually, then sharing with each other. I was the youngest and the least experienced one; Mr. Cynn was the oldest and the wisest of the three, so we went to him for all kinds of questions in connection with the travel.

When the boat docked in Saigon, I watched the coolies loading and unloading cargo. It was winter at home but not here at Saigon. Most of the coolies had no clothes on the upper part of their bodies. Many, clinging to their traditional ways, were wearing braids which got in their way as they worked. "What's the matter with them?" I thought. "Why don't they have their hair cut?" Then the question was pointed at me:

"Who are you that think and say these men should have their hair cut? Why do you cling to your traditions and carry that heavy and unsightly knot on the back of your head all around the world?"

In those days in Korea our hair was considered a symbol of our bodily inheritance from our parents. It belonged to them more than to us, and we were never supposed to treat it lightly or do anything with it without their consent. The only exceptions were the Buddhist nuns, who shaved their heads; and occasionally insane women would have short hair. When the boat docked at Marseilles, the first thing I did after registering at a hotel was to find a barber and have my hair cut. The only thing that troubled me was that I could not tell my parents before doing it. However, upon my return home, both of them told me it was all right. I thought it would shock them, but they were always one step ahead of me.

In Europe we visited the major cities, spending only two or three days in each. But in Denmark we spent two weeks trying to see firsthand the causes and processes of Danish rebirth. The main purpose of the trip for Mr. Hong, the rural secretary, was to study Danish cooperatives. Both the YMCA and YWCA were planning to start a joint project for rural leadership training in Korea, where over eighty percent of the population were farmers. So we were vitally interested in the Danish Folk High Schools. We went to a small-size village, a middle-size one, and to large farms and cities.

The study was so instructive and so inspiring that the next winter we opened a center on the northwestern outskirts of Seoul where the people were living under rural conditions. Training classes for men and women from all over Korea were conducted after the pattern

83

of Danish Folk High Schools, adapted to the Korean situation. Men's classes were held during the winter months, beginning right after the harvest. Women's classes were conducted in the spring, for four to six weeks. Village leaders from all over Korea were beginning to understand and appreciate the meaning of their vocation, and a new spirit was stirring among them. The success of this project was too much for the Japanese authorities to overlook, so after about four years it was abolished. But the historical fact remains that in Korea the YMCA and YWCA had been the pioneers of the village movement, of which Dr. Heung-wu Cynn and Mr. Pyung-sun Hong were the leaders.

At last we arrived at the Mount of Olives where we joined with the other delegates from Korea. I roomed with Miss Dingman from the YWCA of the United States who attended as a staff member of the World Committee. The great people of Christendom seemed to have gathered there, with the towering personality of Dr. John R. Mott as the director-general. The program was all so well arranged, with so much of the preparatory work and papers printed, that the whole thing impressed me tremendously. We lived, worked, and worshiped together for two weeks.

Seeing Dr. Mott preside at the meetings was a great experience all by itself. I looked at him in awe and wonder, for he looked so much like God whom I had seen in a vision when I was sixteen years old. The only difference was that he did not have a beard.

Attending the International Missionary Council in Jerusalem was a mountaintop experience never to be forgotten, and even yet it continues to grow upon me.

In November, 1928, my favorite sister, Ellen, died. She had had tragedies in the loss of her husband and in

the scattering away of her stepsons while in Peking
where her family had gone to live in exile at the time
of annexation. Her health was very poor when she came
with her two small daughters to be with us in Seoul.
We had moved into a house in Ok Chun Dong, still a
small one but a little bit better than the first one in
Song-wol Dong. There was an extra room where sister
could stay with the two girls. We were crowded but
very happy together. Ellen kept on with her studies in
the Chinese classics and would often listen as I sang.
She especially loved to hear "In the City Four Square."
Her death was a heartbreaking sorrow not only for me
but for my two young nieces who already had had more
than they could stand.

The shadow of death seemed to linger around the
corner of our home. In January 1929, father suffered a
brain hemorrhage and died four days later. He had had
such good health that it took us all by surprise. These
experiences made me try to think through once again
the problem of suffering and death. But it was no use;
the more I tried to think, the more I got entangled.
The unknowable should be left alone, and I would do
the best I could with every opportunity in the present
life.

We had a modest funeral for father in Chung Dong
church followed by interment in the city cemetery near
South Mountain. In front of his grave we put up a
memorial stone with a concise record pertaining to his
birth and death. At the end my name was written in
with those of my brothers! This was a deviation from
custom, for daughters' names do not usually appear on
such stones.

In 1944 the Japanese authorities ordered the cemetery
near South Mountain razed and what to do with father's

remains was a serious problem. My cousin, whom father had left on his country homestead, came up to Seoul and moved the remains to our family plot in North Korea, not knowing there ever would be a division of the country.

VI

NEW RESPONSIBILITIES

Friends of Ewha both in Korea and in the United States urged me to go abroad for further studies. The most persuasive of them all was our president, Dr. Alice Appenzeller. When I protested that I had just gotten well into my work and that I wished to stay by it longer before leaving it again, her answer was, "But the college needs faculty members with higher degrees. You could get your doctorate in two years."

I felt I had no choice in the matter. Travel funds and scholarships were provided and as soon as the spring semester was over in 1930, I went to New York City to register for the summer session at Teachers College, Columbia University. My sole aim was to do what I had to do in the shortest time and return to my work at the earliest possible date.

By this time it was quite clear that my lifework would be in the field of higher education, more specifically at Ewha College, training young women for a life of service in Korea. My concern for our rural people and interest in village movements had grown tremendously. As I was facing another opportunity for study there were certain things I wanted to do and to find out. How to make the program for higher education relevant to our new village movement, how to bridge the great chasm between the life of the urban and rural populations, how the educated few could help the underdeveloped people to lift themselves into this new day and age—these were some of my concerns. So the courses I chose at Teachers College included several dealing with rural education. The title for my dissertation was "Rural Education for the Regeneration of Korea." I was taking my courses in English and was doing most of the research for my dissertation in Korean and Japanese. The authorities of Teachers College accepted this as fulfillment of the foreign language requirement instead of insisting upon one or more additional languages, which would have prolonged my stay two or three more years.

Under the professors, who were wonderfully stimulating and sympathetic, I worked with great speed and concentration. Enrolling for the summer sessions as well as the regular terms, I finished the work for the doctorate by October, 1931. Nobody, including myself, could believe that it was all over so soon. My happiness consisted not in the fact of having obtained a higher degree, nor in the fact that I was the first Korean woman with a PhD, but in the fact that I had finished so soon and was ready to return home. I was back at my usual post in the dean's office at Ewha College when the new semester started in January 1932.

Life at Ewha was full and happy and our work was increasing in quality and quantity. The number of applicants for admission to the College was beginning to double and triple. When the first college building, Frey Hall, was built in 1922 our enrollment was under one hundred; and the building was quite adequate. But 1932 presented a different story. More and more students were wanting to enter. Listening to the pleas they made and the stories they told as to why they must be admitted became an unendurable task of the administration. Being the only college for women in all Korea, Ewha could not refuse them and maintain a clear conscience.

Fortunately, our President had already been able to secure funds for the first building on the Sinchon campus, the new site that had been given by Mrs. Gray and her daughter. The donors of the building fund were Mr. and Mrs. Henry Pfeiffer of New York City. After a great deal of preparatory planning, the building was started early in the spring of 1932. For several years the students and faculty had gone to the new site in Sinchon to have picnics, longing for the early construction of our new college buildings. Now our dreams were being translated into brick and stone. For the architectural pattern a modified Gothic style was adopted. The beautiful grayish-white granite was brought from Song-do, which is famous for this stone. At the ground-breaking ceremony and the cornerstone laying, the happy family of students and faculty walked from the old compound to the new campus to thank God for the manifest blessings and to pray for the still-needed unrealized blessings.

In three years' time the first group of buildings was erected: Pfeiffer Hall to house the Literature and Home Economics Departments and the administrative offices, Case Hall for the Music Department and the chapel, and Thomas Gymnasium for physical education. On March 9, 1935, we moved from the impossibly crowded Chung Dong compound to the new, spacious, and beautiful campus in Sinchon.

The ninth of March was the birthday of Miss Frey, the founder of Ewha College, and we chose that day in her honor. The distance between Chung Dong and Sinchon was about two miles. The faculty and entire student body of three hundred marched in procession the whole distance, each carrying something significant to the occasion in her hands. The President and I led

89

the procession, she with the photograph of Mrs. Scranton, the founder of Ewha Haktang, and I with the picture of Miss Frey, the founder of Ewha College. It was quite a walk over the hills, but everyone had light feet and grateful hearts. When we had all arrived, we stood on the front steps of Pfeiffer Hall and had a short service of thanksgiving. As we sang and prayed, thrills went up and down our backs and tears filled our eyes. From that day our new campus was called the Garden of Ewha, meaning the Garden of Eden where God and His children live together.

Before the fall term began, a dormitory was also finished and we did not have to commute from Chung Dong through the winter months. Within a year the Kindergarten Training School with its practice kindergarten moved out to Sinchon where it soon became a department of the College.

May 31, 1936, was the fiftieth anniversary of the founding of Ewha. Although the college work began in 1910, the unclassified first school for girls in all Korea was started on May 31, 1886. It was called Ewha Haktang, and became the mother institution for the elementary, then the secondary, and finally the college divisions. Ewha High School and Ewha Womans University are independent of each other now, but we both celebrate the same founding.

In our celebration that year, the spirit of Ewha was depicted through a pageant entitled "The River," written by Dr. Appenzeller herself. The little beginnings of our history were compared to small streams trickling down through the years and into the large river of Ewha College of the present. This pageant brought out the beauty, the truth, and the goodness sought by Ewha throughout its history. Lighthearted gaiety hovered over all and charmed the audience as the girls sang and played the traditional Korean songs and games. This event signified the setting of a very important milestone on the road of Ewha's progress.

When I returned from America in 1931, my scattered family had reassembled and found a house in Dang-ju Dong. While I was in America, mother had gone to Sunchun where two of my older sisters lived. She came back to Seoul with my nephew, and the two nieces who had been living in the dormitory at Ewha moved back home. Another nephew, my brother's son, joined the family after his father died in the country. So we were a household of six, but the house was big enough for all of us. When my friend Pauline Kim returned from the United States and had no place to stay, she came and occupied the extra room, increasing the family to seven. The location of the house was quite central, making it possible for all of us to commute to schools and places of work. The house also became a meeting place for our group of friends.

One of these close friends was Chungai Lee. She and I had known each other well in our student days at Ewha, but during the intervening years we had gone our separate ways until we came together again in this house. She was working at Severance Nurses' Training School as an assistant director. She saw my need of a close friend, and during her free hours over weekends she always came to help me run the house and make over my old clothes. Friends usually told me that they could tell by my clothes whether Chungai had been with me over the weekend or not. At length we both felt it would be much easier if she moved in and lived with us all the time. After that we shared joy and sorrow, strength and weakness with each other, as good friends

91

should. With the companionship of Pauline and Chungai the house became an abode for friendship.

There was another friend who visited me in this house when she came to Korea. Josephine Brown, who was then the Rural Secretary of the YWCA of China, made a number of professional visits to the Korean YWCA. Miss Ding, the Chinese Executive Secretary, wanted Miss Brown to come over and help with our rural program as well as encourage us in our lonely struggle to build up a fellowship. Her outgoing personality and her capacity for understanding made it possible for us to open our hearts and pour out our troubles. In no time she became a friendly adviser to our new organization. Not only professionally but personally as well she became a staunch friend to many of us. I always looked forward to her coming, for she brought with her the spiritual qualities of hope and enthusiasm, and the YWCA technique of group work in rural and urban situations. Several times she stayed in my home where we had many hours of fellowship and developed a sturdy kind of friendship which has lasted throughout our lives.

Very soon after I returned from Columbia University, President Appenzeller and the Board of Trustees of Ewha asked me to serve as vice-president in addition to my deanship. Dr. Appenzeller insisted that I work with her side by side in all the administrative problems. When her furlough was due in 1936, I was asked to act as president during her absence.

In 1939 the Japanese pressure on our college was asserting itself more and more insidiously. The Japanese authorities had begun to show hostility to all Americans in Korea and finally had come out openly with a ruling that no foreigners should hold the presidency of an educational institution. Dr. Appenzeller resigned and nominated me to succeed her as president.

Very reluctantly I accepted the post. The times were such that under the Japanese domination I knew I could not do any creative piece of work in administration. I also had the fundamental conviction that if one wants to make her best contribution to any group or institution, she has a greater opportunity as a free individual; that is, in a social organization as an ordinary member, in a college faculty as a professor, and in a nation as a plain citizen. Offices and positions condition and limit one by their responsibilities and by the general requirements that one must observe. I never could understand those who either feel very much exalted when they obtain certain positions or very much downhearted when they lose them.

When I expressed this point of view in our discussion, Dr. Appenzeller quoted Shakespeare, "Some are born great, some achieve greatness, and some have greatness thrust upon them." She added, "You are in the third category. You will have to take the presidency whether you like it or not." She stayed by as Honorary President, still helping with the campus development program and assuming more teaching responsibilities.

But Japanese militarism was making a rapid advance in the East and war clouds were gathering all around the Pacific. The United States Consul-General ordered all our missionary personnel to leave the campus on November 16, 1940. As soon as this order was issued, every one of the missionary teachers told me that she was willing to stay and face any consequences. But it was agreed by all concerned that it would be a wise thing for them to depart. There was always the hope of their return when conditions again became normal.

As they were leaving the campus, Dr. Appenzeller held my hand and said, "We are sad to go but glad to leave everything in your hands. We will pray for you and God will take care of you." Against the advice of the police, some of us went down to Inchon to get a last glimpse of our friends before they sailed away on the SS *Mariposa*.

VII

THE BLACK DAYS OF WORLD WAR II

As far as Ewha was concerned, the black days of the Second World War began on November 16, 1940. Returning to the campus from Inchon after saying good-bye to the missionary teachers, I experienced some of the darkest hours of my life. A great sense of loneliness and helplessness almost overwhelmed me. Ewha was still depending upon the subsidies from the missions for its support. Our student enrollment was already over six hundred, but the income from the students was not enough to pay for one third of our expenses. We had no other resources in Korea. How to continue the life of the institution financially, with all our ties with the missions cut away, was the practical problem. In addition there was the Japanese persecution and oppression to face without the support of our missionary colleagues.

As I think back on the part prayer has played in my life, I realize that more than the formal prayers of set times and places, there has been a constant, formless prayer—an attitude of mind that is open to the will and purposes of God. It has been as unconscious and as natural as fish swimming in the sea, as birds flying in the air, as flowers turning to the sun. As soon as I came back and walked into the campus I was fully aware of the presence of Almighty God everywhere, ready to help, comfort, sustain, and continue to bless Ewha and all these who remained with her. From that moment everything was all right, as far as my inner preparation went to fight the battle ahead for Ewha. During those difficult days courage and fortitude, wisdom and guidance were needed daily and hourly from above. We had all these blessings commensurable to our needs.

The news of Pearl Harbor was all over the land on December 7, 1941, about a year after the missionary teachers withdrew. Actual fighting began in the Pacific and the Japanese officials treated Ewha as an enemy institution. They had never been happy with our existence and always found fault with us.

They did not mind the foreigners not being able to speak the Japanese language, but they took it as rebellion when we, the Korean teachers, did not teach in their language. Just before I took the presidency, I saw that I would have to develop more proficiency in the use of Japanese if I were to remain at Ewha. All those years most of us had refused to use it, for that was one of our natural ways of resisting. Now all of us who were not proficient in the Japanese language began to study it and to carry on our work through that medium. Already in the other Korean schools, from primary through college, this rule about the language was strictly observed. Attempts were made to enforce its use even in Korean homes by asking the school children to make daily reports on their parents. To wipe out our Korean language was one phase of the Japanese cultural oppression.

The Japanese authorities had never liked our Home Economics Department, for we insisted on the study of Korean foods and clothing. They would never recognize our graduates as competent enough to teach in our high schools unless they learned Japanese sewing and cooking instead of Korean. The war years gave our oppressors a good pretext for carrying out their designs. All men and women, civilians and students, must wear defense uniforms. Overnight our teachers and students had to dress in shapeless khaki trousers and blouses made of the worst possible material. The garments were too ugly to be in harmony with our campus and spirit. No more Korean sewing, no more fancy Korean cooking, nor anything that was beautiful and representative of Korean culture could be continued.

Right after the beginning of the war we were told not to teach English, for it was the enemy language. All Christian teachings and observances were ruled out. To the Japanese way of thinking, Christianity was no good because it inspired Korean nationalism and an independent spirit. Christian teachings and usage are so allied to the principles of human freedom and dignity that they are inseparable.

Once several Japanese police came without previous notice and went through the girls' rooms in the dormitory. They found hymnbooks and Bibles and used them as evidence of our disobedience to their order. They could not make a case of it, but they scolded us rudely, both the girls and myself, and told us never to use these books again. But the girls sang their songs and I sang mine whenever we could. Some of our favorite hymns were "Simply Trusting Every Day," "Lead, Kindly Light," "Faith of Our Fathers," "I Need Thee Every Hour," and "A Mighty Fortress Is Our God." When we could steal away into a corner where nobody could see or hear us, we sang and prayed as we had never done before. Our strength was renewed, and our fellowship of suffering and faith gave us great comfort.

Among ourselves spoken words were not necessary to understand each other. On occasions when I addressed the student body, I read a prepared speech in the Japanese language. By this time we had several Japanese on our staff, some of whom were government agents.

97

Every word I said was being reported, so I usually had one of them draft my speeches. The content consisted mostly of telling the girls to understand the objectives of the war in the Pacific and to cooperate with the Government. They were all good speeches from the Japanese standpoint, but I knew all the time that the girls were understanding my unspoken words.

But not everybody understood. Even some of my friends and not a few graduates misunderstood and thought that I either loved the position of president enough to keep it at any cost or was really getting pro-Japanese. Some of my close friends would advise me, "You have stood it admirably—so far, but now is the time for you to give up. What is the use of being dragged down into the depths when they won't let you keep your position anyway?" My answer was, "God is still with us; I will not leave." The idea of forsaking Ewha, which had been left in my charge, was unthinkable. My voluntary resignation was just the thing the enemy worked and waited for.

An inspector was formally assigned by the Government to help me preside over Ewha. He came and occupied my office. He called for a faculty meeting and, before my face, said how inadequate I was, being a woman, to be the president. He had come, he said, to assist until I got some adequate help in the person of a Japanese man. He deliberately meant it to be an insult, after which he thought I surely would resign. But I was able to swallow the humiliating pill and instead of resigning thanked him for his offer of help. I also told him I would be glad to welcome a Japanese dean if he could nominate an experienced man with educational qualifications. In the meantime he came to my office every day and made himself at home, inviting our faculty members to come and see him individually. I heard later that he had already been chosen to succeed me before he was sent to us as inspector.

When he left us after ten days, he scolded the men teachers, "You are all cowardly. None of you came to see me because you were afraid of your woman president." The scheme failed and the Japanese did not get rid of me as easily as had been anticipated.

The Japanese dean, Mr. Komoto, was, to our good fortune, a real gentleman who had a great deal of sympathy for and understanding of what was going on in Ewha. As soon as he arrived and took hold of the situation, he worked with me very closely. He surprised both the Japanese group within the college and in the government Bureau of Education. He was not going to work as their agent. Rightly and justly he respected my views and stood up for them. They called him the President's man, but he did not mind. Mutual respect and confidence helped us to establish a beautiful working relationship in no time.

We were getting along nicely until another scheme was devised to upset us. This time it was the complete change of our curriculum. The normal program of higher education must all be stopped. Carry on only a one-year course for the training of village leaders—this was our new order. The village leaders were not to be used for village enlightenment or social and economic improvement, but only for Japan's war purposes. The girls were all to scatter over Korea's rural communities and tell the people about the war and what they must do to help win it.

When the time for registration arrived, only forty girls came; and we had so little to do that we planted trees on the hillsides. The girls who graduated and went out to the villages were very specifically instructed to carry on classes composed of young adult women under the supervision of the Japanese principals of the public schools. Their classes were all to be conducted in the Japanese language. The girls reported to us after a year that they had wonderful experiences in their work. When they visited the students in their homes, they could talk in Korean and communicate their real purposes.

We were ordered to change the name of the college since the name Ewha was associated with so many "bad traditions." Henceforth the name was to be Kyung-Sung Woman's College. We all wept when we sang our Ewha college song together for the last time, even though we were singing it in the Japanese translation.

Not only the institution, but we personally had to change our names. In their thoroughgoing process of wiping out our identity, our oppressors felt that they might make us into real Japanese if our names were changed. There is a great deal of difference between Korean and Japanese names. Korean names are usually monosyllables such as Kim, Lee, Pak, Choi, Ahn; while Japanese names are of two, three, or four syllables such as No-wa, Ya-na-gi, Ku-ma-mo-to.

Only a few Korean individuals of great importance could survive without accepting this change of name. In my case pressure was brought to bear by saying, "You must set a good example within the College as president and in society as a public leader." To me this was the most difficult thing to do. I had received my name from my father who was not living to be consulted. With me, this was not a national or patriotic issue but a very personal one of loyalty to my deceased father. The final date was approaching and I had to make the decision.

Fortunately I had a friend well versed in Japanese names. He did some research and found one "least objectionable," as he put it. He sensed and understood my feelings about the change. "I have selected Amagi, the name of a very good Japanese author," he said. "It means 'heavenly city.'" Instantly I replied, "Good, I will take that name. In the heavenly city it doesn't matter what one is called. Father, who is already there, would approve it." My Korean name Whallan means the same as Katsuran in Japanese. So until liberation I was called Amagi Katsuran, meaning the "living orchid of heavenly city." "Since you had to change, we are glad you have such a nice name," my friends said.

One good thing that happened to Ewha during this dark period was the organization of the Legal Holding Body. Due to our origin, our land and other properties were held by the Methodist Board of Missions. This involved problems for us and we should have had an independent legal organization long before. We needed cash assets in order to obtain government recognition of the Legal Body. Our properties were more than adequate but there was not a cent of cash. A benefactress, Mrs. Tai-Kyung Chu, was found in Wonsan. She listened to the appeal and gave her lifelong savings of one hundred thousand *won,* a large sum at the time and the very first large gift from a Korean woman. But even this was not sufficient. Mr. Chang-sik Sohn of Shanghai was another benefactor who appeared on our horizon. He heard about our need and gave five hundred thousand *won,* the largest sum ever contributed by a Korean. With these two gifts we were able to register our Legal Holding Body, an incorporated body financially responsible for the College. This accomplishment was another milestone in the development of Ewha College.

Even after all their repressive measures were taken, Ewha under my leadership did not present a happy situation to the Japanese authorities. In April 1944, they took over the Christian College for men in our neighborhood and we were informed that a whole delegation was coming out to take us over too. They were sure they would find enough faults with our accounts to cause me to resign.

Early in the morning they came to go through all our books and accounts. I met them at the station and escorted them to the College. As we walked into the campus, the stately buildings glistened in the morning sun against the pine-clad hillsides. They kept saying, "Wonderful! Wonderful campus!" A short distance from the entrance the director of the Bureau of Education looked up at the handsome willow tree, about two hundred years old, and exclaimed, "What a fine tree!" Immediately I pointed out to him a small willow tree we had planted that spring close by the old one and said, "Look at that young one. It's there to grow and eventually take the place of the old. The main trunk of the big one already shows signs of decay." His mood changed and his face turned solemn. I never knew whether he got my point or not. I wanted him to know that we were set for posterity and that we intended to stand firm and immovable.

The entire group of about twelve men worked hard all day prying into everything connected with our business management. They found nothing against us; instead, they found not only the absence of any irregularities but also many facts in our favor. They saw how meager our income was, but how far we were stretching it to count the most for the College. They found that there had not been enough funds for me to draw any salary after the mission appropriations were cut off, and that I had sold my home and was using the money for the College and to sustain my family. They found out that from our meager funds I never failed to pay the salaries of teachers and employees on time.

These facts impressed, moved, and inspired the key man in the group. He testified later that he could not hurt me any more, so secretly decided to help me. That night as they were discussing the events of the day and what to do next, he discreetly led the decision to leave me on trial a little longer since they had found nothing to blame me for. From that day he stood and fought for me and I was able to keep my charge to the last.

In the meantime the Japanese military authorities were taking measures to meet Japan's war needs. They began to conscript our Korean youth, some for the regular army but most for civilian labor. All metal attached to or used in buildings was being taken. Our Ewha buildings were not exceptions, and they were stripped of all the iron railings outside and brass decorations inside. Our sadness was multiplied one day when we heard that the Underwood statue at Chosen Christian College, now Yonsei University, and the copper plaques of our Ewha founders, Mrs. Scranton and Miss Frey, had to be given up.

With our student body so small, we had no way to refuse when the request came through the Bureau of Education for space for the Army. We quickly set up a temporary hospital in Pfeiffer Hall to avoid turning it over to the soldiers. I moved into Longview, the missionary residence on the campus, to keep the officers out. Dean Komoto and his family lived in the English Practice House. We were using Case Hall for most of our work, and the girls were still in the dormitory. The

Army occupied our gymnasium and the education building only. We had very strict agreements to limit the military personnel to these two buildings and their surrounding grounds.

My friend, Chungai Lee, was taking care of the dormitory girls. Her difficulties and problems were already insurmountable. Where to find enough food supplies and how to pay for them were her concerns. The frequent visits of the police for surveillance, and the nightly yelling of the defense officials when light chanced to leak through the window of a careless girl were breaking down her health. When the Japanese soldiers came onto the campus, so near the girls' dormitory, it was the last straw and she broke down completely. She had competent help in Okgill Kim, and we all pitched in to keep watch night and day over the welfare of the girls. Somehow Chungai revived and went back to her work.

We had just one bad incident. A couple of soldiers off duty, partly drunk, came around to the back of the dormitory and called to the girls, throwing stones at them and trying to crawl over the roof to break through the window. With this breach of agreement, we demanded the prompt withdrawal of the soldiers from our buildings. The officers and even higher authorities apologized and promised that never again would such a thing happen. They did abide by this promise to the end, and it was our turn to show them compassion when they withdrew quietly after the defeat.

Toward the end of the war as the situation got increasingly tense, the Japanese used a "divide and rule" policy among the leaders of our society. Hardly any organizations had survived except the Christian churches. Any number of spies were used to intimidate and tempt our Christian leaders to suspect each other, creating factions within the churches. The agents would pretend to favor a certain leader and would give him a chance to exercise power over the church to which he belonged. They made up imaginary cases of independence activities and arrested the suspected leaders, who were severely beaten to force them to make false confessions. Some never survived these trials.

Once I was caught among these false charges. One of my former friends gave the Japanese my name because, as he told me afterward, he had to tell them something. For three days in succession I was called to the police station to be questioned all day. They subjected me to many personal indignities. With all kinds of intimidations and wiles they tried to force me into a false confession that I was a member of a secret organization. Each time I answered with clarity and finality that I knew of the existence of no such organization. "Ewha College, YWCA, and the church are the only institutions I belong to. Please leave me alone if they are not objectionable ones to you," was my only answer.

Some weeks after the atom bombs were dropped on Hiroshima and Nagasaki, we were told that over ten thousand leaders in Korean society who had been kept on the blacklist of the Japanese police were to have been arrested. In case of eventual Japanese defeat, the authorities thought these Koreans would become leaders and would retaliate against them. They had planned to massacre this group about the fifteenth of August, which proved to be the very day of the Japanese surrender.

If the atom bombs hastened the surrender, we who were on the blacklist feel that they spared our lives. While we mourn for the loss of innocent lives, ever so many more than were on our list, we cannot help noticing the historic coincidence as such.

105

VIII

LIBERATION

We were hardly breathing under the double yoke of a
foreign rule and the last stage of a losing war, when
the faltering voice of the Japanese emperor came over
the radio announcing his surrender at noon, August
15, 1945. What news! We could hardly take it in at
once. Dean Komoto was with us when we heard it in
my office. As he was leaving the room he said, "How
well the authorities deceived us!" We knew he meant
that the government information about the war had
been all wrong. We said to each other, "This means
liberation, freedom, and independence for us!" We
could not sit still, and ran out to the streets to have
the news confirmed and reconfirmed, and in our turn
telling everyone on the way.

People were on the streets by the thousands all
through the night. They were waving Korean flags and
yelling *Mansei*. The streetcars and buses were rolling up
and down with students and other citizens waving, clap-
ping, and congratulating each other. They shouted
Mansei and sang the long-forbidden national song. The
experience of this great joy of liberation was so overwhelming and so cleansing that no Korean attacked a
Japanese in retaliation. No one slept that night or on
many succeeding nights. After a little catnap we would
awake, startled, then jump up saying, "We are free! We
are free!"

The day after the surrender, I walked the streets to
find out what was being done for the maintenance of
order and security. Still the streets were dominated by

106

the hilarious masses, and the prospective leaders were all unavailable. In the central part of the city on one of the school grounds Mr. Woon-hyung Lyuh was having a meeting of the so-called Reconstruction Preparatory Committee. Mr. Lyuh was one of our national leaders who worked abroad as an exile in China and Manchuria. He had returned to Korea and had been identified with sports circles, and was very well liked. The grounds were so packed with people that I could not get near. The crowd seemed unruly and disorganized. I was half puzzled as to whether anything constructive could come out of such a meeting and half satisfied to know that preparations were under way by some people to take control of the situation. By the time I returned home in the late afternoon, statements and orders had begun to be issued in the name of this committee.

But very soon a strange thing began to happen which disillusioned and saddened us. Our leaders who had hitherto been united in their common resistance against the colonial rule were now divided against each other. Some were on the right, some on the left, and some in between. The people wanted a united leadership, but the leaders could not or would not unite. Similar situations prevailed on college campuses among both students and faculty. Grand confusion resulted in institutions and in society in general.

However, the worst blow of all was the division of the land into North and South at the thirty-eighth parallel. We just stumbled onto the fact, for we were never consulted or even told why and how this division had come into existence.

We thought that the Russian army in the North and the American army in the South were coming in separately only for the purpose of receiving the Japanese surrender. But soon the line was frozen as though Korea had suddenly become a battleground. Our leaders and relatives who were above the line fled South, telling tales hard to believe in regard to the situation prevailing in the North, where a communist government was being formed. Over three million people crossed the line, leaving their homes and possessions, and often members of their families, because they preferred living in freedom in the South. Many perished on the way, but others kept coming until they were stopped by the armies stationed on both sides of the line.

Then we heard that a Joint Commission was to be formed, with representatives of both the American and Russian commands and of Koreans from both zones to work out a plan to establish a united and independent Korea. Our hopes rose again, but two things puzzled the minds of the people. The first was why the leaders of the two armies assumed that the division of the country was an accomplished fact. The whole world was talking about a divided Korea, but the Koreans had not known anything about it. We were one homogeneous race, one land, one economy, one language and culture, and had suffered as one people under the Japanese. Was Korea to be used again as a pawn in the power struggle between the strong nations?

The second puzzling question in our minds was why none of our leaders or groups who had been working for our independence in the States and elsewhere had known about the partition. Were they not consulted? Why had they not found out and stopped such a cruel and unnecessary division? It must have been done under some international agreement.

In October 1945, Dr. Syngman Rhee returned to Korea. But even he did not seem to know how it happened and how we could reunite. Up to the present time no one has even attempted to give us an answer or an explanation, let alone an apology. We only acquiesce and suffer the consequences of this wrong which must have come from the maladjustments made in international relations following the war.

The repeated attempts of the Joint American-Soviet Commission to reach an agreement ended each time in total failure. Then came the suggestion for a trusteeship as an interim agreement until an independent Korea could be established. Once again the populace was excited and enraged. Intelligentsia, laborers, students, men and women in groups and as individuals took to the streets expressing in no uncertain terms their horror and indignation at the suggestion. Virtually all but the Communists opposed it.

At every crisis in the life of the nation ever since the Independence Movement of 1919, women have played an important role. We decided as a women's group to do our share in this struggle. Early on a January morning in 1946, when the weather was bitter cold, with snow and ice on the ground, women paraded with placards through the streets of Seoul and stood in line in front of the Government building. The placards read, "No trusteeship, only independence," "Our opposition to trusteeship is absolute," "Why replace one master with many?" "No more alien rule; we want independence." We were determined not to leave our positions until our expressions were taken seriously and relayed to the proper authorities.

When I came home on the night of the third day of our demonstrations, a notice from General John R. Hodge, the American Military Commander in Seoul, was waiting. He asked me to come to his office the next morning. I had no idea what he wanted.

Dr. Myomook Lee, his interpreter, escorted me into his office. Our interview was short and to the point. At once he said, "We know you do not want trusteeship. I have already made reports to that effect to my superiors. Will you tell your women to go back to their homes and to their work and not to walk or stand on the streets in the cold?" He showed displeasure and provocation at the activities of the women. I tried to answer him, stating that we were simply representing the sentiment of the entire people and that we wanted to make sure that he understood our feelings. He assured me that he did and dismissed me, and that was the last we heard of that!

Since no solution for the reunification and independence of Korea had been reached by the Joint Commission, the United States delegation submitted the problem to the General Assembly of the United Nations. The United Nations resolution, as finally passed over the opposition of the Soviet delegation, called for the creation of a Temporary Commission on Korea.

This Temporary Commission was dispatched to Korea to supervise the election of representatives to a National Assembly and to assist in setting up a unified national government. We were willing to cooperate to the maximum extent. However, the Temporary Commission made repeated attempts to enter the northern territory, but were refused every time. At length the Temporary Commission reported the situation to the United Nations and were directed to authorize and supervise general elections in the area accessible to them. The responsibility for the conduct of the elections rested with the United States Military Command. It was the general estimate at the time that about two-thirds of our population was in the South while less than one-third remained in the North. Since so much time had already been lost in the futile effort to have the Northern Command come to any reasonable agreement, we welcomed this move of the United Nations Temporary Commission to carry on general elections in the accessible area alone.

For the first time in Korean history people were given an opportunity to exercise the franchise. The National Assembly was to be composed of one representative to every one hundred thousand people. This would make a total number of about three hundred. We were roughly estimating our population to be thirty million, twenty in South Korea and ten in the North. In this general election we would have only the representatives of the southern population, since one-third of the seats in the Assembly would be left vacant to be filled whenever similar elections could take place in the North. Everybody was happy and busy getting ready for the elections to be held on May 10, 1948.

Only two days prior to the deadline for the registration of candidates, representatives of women's groups came and begged me to run for election. I said, "No, I have my hands full with the work at the college; and I have never wanted to enter into active politics." They would not give up but insisted that I do it for the sake of all women in Korea even if I personally did not care to. I prophesied that no woman was going to be elected and that they would be disappointed at the outcome. They persisted that this was the very first time women were to be on equal terms with men. "If you are not a candidate and no woman is elected, we will always blame you for not having stood up for the rights of women. If you are not elected, we will know that our society has granted equality on paper only, not in practice. At least we would have done our best and not have given up our rights without trying."

Under these circumstances I felt again that I had no choice. I agreed to let the women submit my name. I also learned that eighteen other women from all over the country were running for election. We women all worked together from that day. Unwilling as I had been in the beginning, I made a sincere effort to win votes.

We learned many things from our experience in this first election. As soon as we had made the decision to run for election, all the women candidates met together and agreed upon some principles for campaigning. The fundamental principle was that we would conduct an exemplary campaign. In order to do this we would not make it a costly project. We would not express or entertain any malicious feelings toward our rivals. We would strictly adhere to the truth when we spoke. We would make our bills and posters look attractive. Through this opportunity we would generate good feeling and appreciation for truth and beauty all about us.

The last few days we rode through the city on a truck decorated with beautiful cloth and flowers until it looked like a float. Our campaigning women wore pretty clothes and some of us spoke and sang through the loudspeakers in melodious harmony. Although, as we had foreseen, not a single woman was elected, we had the joy and satisfaction of having had a clean and beautiful campaign.

We might have won if our rivals had not at the last minute spread distorted facts and imaginary tales against me among the less educated people around the outskirts of Seoul who were not able to discriminate

112

between truth and falsehood. Even so, the number of votes cast for me was the second highest of those cast for the eight candidates receiving support from the areas where the intelligentsia lived.

The night when the votes were being counted, I slept soundly and greatly irritated my friends, who sat up all night and listened for the radio news of the results. I did not think my sitting up would help any; morning was early enough for me to know the results. After breakfast I went over to the office of my successful rival and congratulated him on the election. He was Mr. Do-yun Kim, one of my three Korean friends during the first year at Ohio Wesleyan.

The first National Assembly in our history convened on May 31, 1948, and elected Dr. Syngman Rhee as its first chairman. The first constitution of the country was promulgated on July 17, 1948. Under the new constitution, Dr. Syngman Rhee was elected as the first president of the new Republic of Korea. His inauguration marked the formal beginning of the independent nationhood of our country. We all wept for joy at witnessing this rebirth of our nation, at the same time conscious of the deep sorrow within our hearts for the division of the country and the consequent absence of ten million of our people held as captives of the Communists. We dedicated ourselves anew to the reclamation of our land and people in the North.

To go back three years, soon after liberation we decided at Ewha to make our new start as a university rather than to continue as a college. We were free to do as we thought best since we were no longer dominated by an alien government. There was already the basis for a university, since several departments could be grouped into colleges. Not to make too large a beginning, we

113

reorganized the curriculum and constructed a university with three colleges: the College of Liberal Arts and Science, the College of Music and Fine Arts, and the College of Healing Arts which comprised premedical and medical courses, nursing education, and pharmacy. We set the date for this grand new start for October, 1945.

We assembled the necessary documents and filed our application for registration with the American Military Government, in which the chief of the Ministry of Education was an army captain. He was a good man who knew how to work with the Korean Advisory Committee on Education. I was on the Committee and enjoyed working with him. We had frequent meetings, almost daily at times. There was no transportation and I had to walk about three miles all the way from Sinchon to the government buildings. But it was a joyous task and I did not complain.

Then all of a sudden, representatives of the U.S. Army Medical Corps appeared on the campus late in August and demanded that I evacuate the college in five days. They had looked over the entire country to find the most suitable place for an army hospital and had decided upon the Ewha campus. In spite of my protests that we were preparing to reopen as a university in October, they were adamant. I asked them to arrange a conference for me to see and talk directly to their superiors. This they grudgingly agreed to, although they told me with much authority and finality that I would have to obey the order to evacuate the campus.

I was at my wits' end when out to our campus came Harold Isaacs, a *Newsweek* correspondent. He had heard about the Army plan to take our campus. I poured out all my troubles to him and he promised to help.

On the day of my appointment with the head of the Medical Corps, Mr. Isaacs managed to find transportation and took me to the building. On the way he told me to speak out all my thoughts and feelings. He was ready to wire to American papers in case we were forced to surrender the campus against our wishes. He would say that the American Army took over Ewha College, the only mission college for girls, against the desire of its Korean president, Dr. Helen Kim. Although I was helpless, as a foreign correspondent he had a weapon to use for us.

We arrived and I was escorted into the General's headquarters. The officers who had been to see me before were present. I told the General a little bit about the history of Ewha—who had founded it, what we had gone through during the war years, how jubilant we were in getting ready to make a new start, and what a blow it was to be told to evacuate. I asked him some questions: "Would you ask an American woman's college to evacuate for the Army? Can you confiscate private property for army use even after the war has ceased?" His answer was, "No, we do not want to confiscate it. That is why we are asking for your consent."

He told me how hard they had looked all over Korea for a place and how fortunate they felt when they found our buildings equipped with a heating system. "Winter will be here in no time and we need a place where sick soldiers can be taken care of. It will be their first winter in an unaccustomed climate, which may mean a large number of pneumonia cases. Won't you let us use your campus? We will help you to find another place, to fix it up, and to move. We will do all we can for you."

It was very difficult to say no when he put it up to me like that, but I felt I had to answer in the negative.

115

"Ewha is public property belonging to all Korean women and entrusted to me for a specific purpose," I said. "All our graduates, present students, and their parents would wish me to continue the college work there. It is a hard thing to say, but my answer has to be no. You have the resources to build a new place much more easily than I could ever hope to." At the end of the conversation the General said he would let me know his decision.

I left the place and went back to the campus. Mr. Isaacs stayed on and waited for the outcome. Later in the day he came out to Ewha and told me that the Army had decided not to take our campus. The next day the official notice of this decision was brought to me. Another crisis at Ewha was averted.

Years later I could forget my former anxiety and smile when Mrs. Douglas Horton told how angry those medical officers had been at my refusal. She heard them talking about it in Tokyo, where she was a member of the first Education Mission to Japan after the war. They were blaming the missions saying, "Missionaries have no business to go abroad and train people who can be so articulate in the English language."

True to our plan, on October 1, 1945, we opened the first academic year of Ewha Womans University with nine hundred students in the three colleges. Our surroundings had not changed much. There were the same hillsides, the same buildings, and many of the former faculty members. Our elated feelings as free people made us live and work as if in the clouds. Our enthusiasm knew no bounds, and the blessings of freedom outweighed any difficulties. The new Ewha University sailed on full steam in its course during the first year.

The Ministry of Education of the Military Government was very slow with our registration as a university. They found fault with our papers, which we promptly corrected according to their directions. But weeks and months passed without final action. Only on August 15, 1946, was the registration granted as a special gift on the first anniversary of our liberation. We rejoiced, for we had waited almost a year. Later we suspected the real reason for the delay. In a man's country how could a woman's university be registered as the very first? The two men's universities, Yonsei (Chosen Christian University) and Korea University, had been slow in presenting their applications. Obviously our papers had to wait until those of the two men's institutions were complete. They were registered as numbers one and two. Our registration number was three. This illustrates the constant battle women have to make for recognition of any sort. We were glad to be even number three, but justly resented the unfair delay.

In early February, 1946, I was invited to go to the National Convention of YWCA. It was urgent that Korea be represented at this meeting after so long a separation. But there were no boats or planes for civilians. I appealed to the American Army and they flew me out. It was my first airplane ride, and my first return to the United States after fifteen years.

The very evening I landed in Atlantic City I had to appear on the platform of the Convention. As I stood there and looked at my friends of YWCA, my feeling of joy and gratitude was overwhelming. I sensed in response a similar feeling from the audience as I told them how great was the appreciation of our women for freedom and our gratitude to the American Army which had fought to liberate us. I was able also to present the jewels that our women had sent. These jewels were family heirlooms. Our women could not contain their joy at liberation. They had to do something, so they opened up their family treasures and sent the best of their jewels as an expression of their joy and gratitude to American women for the victory that their sons and husbands had won.

I found that the American public was not ready to hear and understand what the Communists were doing in North Korea. The people were sympathetic to Korea but at the same time felt the Russians had been their allies in the war, and they wanted to remain friends. Any stories not complimentary to their allies they did not wish to hear, keeping their eyes blinded to the realities of communism. On the other hand, some people surprised me by criticizing several of our outstanding men, such as our revered leaders Sung-soo Kim and Chin-wu Song. Such men and women had kept the resistance movement within Korea going and had kept the hope of freedom shining all through the dark days. Mr. Sung-soo Kim became the second vice-president after our Republic was established. I saw that just as in Korea after liberation, there was division here too. In the realm of political thought, some leaned to the left, some to the right.

One of my sad discoveries on this trip was that my dear friend, Miss Florence Gibson, had died. She had been my American mother ever since I came to study in the United States in 1922. She had made many sacrifices in order to make my stay in the United States more comfortable and fruitful. A strong bond of love grew between us through the years. But during the war communications were not possible. The first and only letter received from her after the war had been in January, 1946. She wrote me to come as soon as possible, for she

118

might not have too long a time left in this world. I did go as fast as I could, but it was too late; for she had died about two weeks before my arrival. I went to her home in Washington, D.C., and to the cemetery in Muncy, Pennsylvania, where she was buried. Still I could not accept the fact of her death, although I found her gone physically. Then as I was thinking and praying in the hotel room in Muncy, a keen sense of her presence was felt. There was a real communion of her spirit and mine. I could come away comforted and strengthened.

In the fall of 1946 the evacuated missionary teachers began to return. Once again the helpful exchange of East and West at Ewha was restored. In 1940 we had been separated with tears of sorrow; in 1946 we were rejoined with tears of happiness. Dr. Alice Appenzeller had waited at the nearest place, Honolulu, and was the first to return. Then others—Miss Marion Conrow, Miss Ana B. Chaffin, Miss Marie Church, Miss Jeannette Hulbert, Miss Ada B. Hall, Miss Clara Howard, Miss Grace Wood—followed. Only those who had passed the age limit for retirement failed to return. Dr. Appenzeller and the others all took their full schedules for teaching the subjects they had formerly taught, mostly in the field of English language and literature. Life at Ewha was fast returning to happy and normal conditions, with promising new developments.

Then on February 20, 1950, Dr. Appenzeller became ill as she was leading the chapel service. I was a little late and had sat down on the back row as she read the scripture lesson. When she began her message, I noticed a change coming over her countenance as well as in her speech. I went swiftly but quietly up to the platform and stood beside her as she tried to continue. I said to her, "I think you are not well, let us go down." She gave up

119

reluctantly, insisting that she must finish her talk, but when I tried to help her walk back, she was already unable to move.

We dismissed the students and carried her to a couch in the reception room. When the doctors arrived she could not speak at all. As she was being carried on a stretcher from the reception room to the ambulance which was to take her to Severance Hospital, she moved her right hand as if trying to grasp something. I took hold of her hand and she held mine tightly until we were ready to close the ambulance door. She was not able to speak, but I knew this last handclasp meant exactly the same thing she had said as she held my hand when she had to evacuate in 1940. "I am sorry to go, but glad to leave everything in your hands. I will pray for you and God will help you."

She died soon after reaching the hospital. We clothed her in a pure white Korean dress and laid her body away in the Yang-Wha-Do Foreign Cemetery after a beautiful funeral service in Chung Dong church. She was the first Western baby born in Korea and had been baptized in this church. So many came to pay their last homage to her that the church was overcrowded and we had to install a loudspeaker for the large number who were standing outside. On her tombstone we inscribed her Wellesley College motto which she had kept as hers all through her life, "Not to be ministered unto but to minister."

The life and work of Alice Appenzeller left a lasting impact upon the lives of many graduates of Ewha and upon the institution itself. With her continuous blessings from beyond, the University's expanding life continued.

IX

THE KOREAN WAR AND EXILE

At four o'clock on the morning of June 25, 1950, we began to hear in the distance the strange pounding of big guns, then the sound of hundreds and thousands of rifles nearby. The North Korean armed forces were attacking across the thirty-eighth parallel.

With the inauguration of the Republic of Korea in 1948 the country began to develop in all phases of its national life. Although there was still need for postwar adjustments, being a liberated people we had a new spirit and zeal for life. We made progress in reconstruction of bridges, railroads, schools, industry, and waterpower. But the Northern army knew how unprepared our military forces were. The U. S. Army had withdrawn earlier in the year and we had only the beginnings of a small constabulary force for security purposes. The Communists in the North must have been making plans all along to capture the whole of Korea, and they must have calculated that the sooner they struck the better their chances were to win.

The radio promptly began to inform us that the Northern army was invading the South and was already attacking with full force all along the dividing line at the thirty-eighth parallel. Our forces were doing everything possible to keep the invading army from advancing. Citizens were asked to stay at their posts, ready and willing to cooperate with the Government forces. We did not know what to do or where to turn. During the night all the missionary personnel were evacuated by the United States embassy.

Early in the forenoon I went to the Ministry of Defense to get firsthand information and decide what to do at the college in this crisis. On the streets and at the Ministry the scenes were pathetic. Officers were gathering up untrained soldiers to be dispatched in any available vehicles to the front lines, which were then within thirty miles of Seoul. I learned that at some points the enemy had already penetrated far into our territory. I fully sensed how urgent the crisis was and how immediate the danger.

Next I hurried to the Ministry of Education and found that a conference was called for that afternoon. I went back to Ewha and called a meeting with colleagues to discuss how to take care of the students, particularly the three hundred girls in the dormitory, and how best to serve the country and the people. Refugees were already coming into the city from the battle area. We postponed our final decisions until after the meeting at the Ministry.

In the afternoon meeting clear thinking was already difficult. The consensus was that we all should stand by and keep our positions in order to show our high morale and national patriotism. I protested that hundreds of girls lived in the dormitory at Ewha. Who would guarantee their safety? They must be sent home immediately. To this I received a very challenging response from the Minister, Dr. George Paik, "If Ewha did that, it would result in a breakdown of the morale of the other schools and eventually of the people as a whole. Please keep the students on the campus and we will all help you take care of them."

About six o'clock in the morning of the twenty-seventh, Miss Kyum Sook Pak, a graduate of Ewha, called on the phone and told me to leave the city at once. From her I learned that both the national and the city governments had moved to Suwon during the night and that all the Ministers had left before dawn, saying they would be back in three days. Without telling a word to the people, all the responsible leaders had left the city. Not only this, but through the radio the citizens were still being told to keep their places and go about their ordinary business, for the enemy was being driven back.

We immediately declared temporary recess of the school. Without hesitation we sent the dormitory students to their homes on the morning trains. We posted men at each entrance to the campus to tell the day students to go back home and stay until notified. The faculty and staff were asked to do whatever they could on or off the campus. A group of us were thinking of plans to receive and care for refugees, but they were not coming our way. The exodus was southward across the Han river bridge, while our campus was on the northwestern outskirts of the city.

I went into the city in the afternoon to size up the situation. Guns and rifles were roaring nearby and enemy planes were already strafing the city. It was not safe to be on the streets. I went to Chungai's sister's house and sat by the radio. The message kept saying that we were gaining in the battle and that we should keep our posts. As I was returning to the campus for the night, the chief of the police station nearby came running to my jeep and whispered that I must leave. When I told him what the radio was saying, he said, "Nonsense! The enemy is nearing Don-Am-Dong!" This is in the northeastern part of the city. "Go home and get some supper," he added, "then leave. Lose no time." By leaving I would make the security problem easier for our neighborhood police chief, since I would undoubtedly be suspect to the Communists. Since I had no work to do temporarily, I decided that I would follow the Government and do what I could to help the cause of the nation.

When I returned home my two housemates, lulled by the information from the radio, were playing a game. Around the supper table I told them what I had seen and heard in the city. They both felt that I should leave at once. Chungai Lee, the director of the Nursing Department, said she would remain with the keys for the whole campus. Youngyi Kim, director of the Music Department, said she would take me to her home in Suwon twenty-five miles south of Seoul. I changed my clothes quickly, picked up my devotional diary, and was ready to go. Chungai handed me some money, and Youngyi and I left about 6:30, telling Chungai that we would be back in three days. In the meantime the driver filled up the jeep with some gasoline Chungai had put away. Gasoline was more precious than blood after the war got started. The jeep driver did not even have a chance to say good-bye to his family. It was raining miserably.

It was after seven when our jeep reached the Han river bridge. The military police told us we could not pass because we did not have an order from the President. "At a time like this how could the President be bothered with individual passes?" I snapped back. "He and the Government have gone down to Suwon, so I am following. Isn't that enough reason to let me pass?" As the police were still blocking my way, a soldier who had been supervising nearby recognized me and stepped up, suggesting that I could go and ask the commander of the group for permission. The commander not only gave permission to go across the river but also took all the precautionary measures not to have us sent back at any of the checking points.

We arrived at Suwon about ten o'clock and had a good night's rest. The first news we received in the morning was that the Han river bridge had been bombed and that the Communists had taken our capital city of Seoul. Our hearts sank. Nothing worse could have happened to us as individuals or to our nation! What about our friends, colleagues, students, and families who were all caught in the trap! Youngyi and I looked at each other, and wept. Our immediate impulse was to return to Seoul, but no one was allowed to go back. We were told that the Government had gone on further down to Taejon and that we should move on too.

We had to follow the order of the day and go southward, the opposite direction from where we wanted to go. The sights we saw were heartbreaking. Dazed and weary soldiers were everywhere, trying to get to their positions. Some did not seem to know where they were going. This was already the fourth day of the war. They had had no sleep and no food all that time. Some were lying on the roadside dead, or motionless from sheer exhaustion. For the first time in my life I regretted not being a man who could turn right around and go to the front to fight. Not being able to do that I resolved within my heart that I would do anything and everything I could to help with the war in which those boys had fought till exhaustion or death. This determination burned within my soul all during the war years. It is still burning, for the war has not ended yet.

Down in Taejon a good Christian friend, Elder Lee, welcomed us into his home. Contact was made with our friends in the Ministry, Defense Minister Sung-mo Syn and Education Minister George Paik. They explained why they had had to leave all of a sudden and had not been able to give me even a telephone call. It was understandable, for overwhelming events were taking place daily and hourly. I sent word to President Rhee that I had followed the Government and that I was available for any work that a woman could do in time of war.

The news reached us in Taejon of the prompt action of the United Nations Security Council in dispatching a collective force to stop the unprovoked aggression of the Communists. By July 1, companies of the twenty-fourth division of the United States Army under General William F. Dean were already arriving from Japan. But our battleline was being pushed back. On July 15 the Keum river fell into the hands of the enemy and by July 17 they had reached the outskirts of Taejon. On July 20, the twenty-fourth division withdrew its rear guard from Taejon and two days later General Dean was reported missing.

In the meantime our Government had moved down to Taegu and the next day Defense Minister Syn had sent word for Youngyi and me to leave the city. We were to go to Mokpo and report to Captain Choon-mo Chung who was in command of that harbor. It had been not more than a week since we had arrived in Taejon. Again Youngyi and I started out in our jeep toward Mokpo. Parts of the road were flooded and it was still raining. Our driver, Insoo Kim, was grieving that his wife and family had been left behind. He had not even had time to tell his wife where he was going when we left Seoul.

When we reached Mokpo, Captain and Mrs. Chung were expecting us and welcomed us royally. We stayed in their home for fifteen days and were not subjected to any of the discomforts which most refugees faced. They even had new clothes made for us, for we needed a change. We became such good friends that they adopted me as their godmother. But no word came of family and friends in Seoul, and we sorrowed deeply.

One day a call came from President Rhee for me to go to Pusan immediately and take responsibility for the Red Cross administration. The only way to go was by boat, and Captain Chung arranged for us to travel on an army transport ship. After eight hours at sea, we were told that we must go back to Mokpo on account of danger ahead from enemy vessels. On a second try we went through and arrived at Pusan port safely. Governor and Mrs. Sung-Bong Yang of Kyung Sang Province met us and took us to their official residence. Here again we had no worry for daily provisions, and Mrs. Yang made me a pair of pale khaki-colored trousers and a light short-sleeved blouse as a working outfit. This served me well all summer.

At the Red Cross headquarters there was much to do. Volunteer women reported for work until the rooms became so crowded that we had to tell some to stay at home until we had more space. Many took work to their homes, for bandages and bedclothes were needed without limit. Medicines were coming in from all parts of the world for the wounded and sick. Staff members and volunteers were busy receiving, sorting, and dispatching these supplies to needy places. There was such demand that we had to have a priority list all the time.

What I was very anxious about was the food situation in Seoul where all our people were caught unawares. I appealed to the army and other authoritative quarters to drop some food from the air to keep the Seoul popu-

lace from starving. It seemed to me that in the name of
the Red Cross other countries might participate in such
a plan for meeting human need. I was told that there
was no way of making sure that the food we might drop
would get to the needy people and that populations
usually could survive through such a siege at least three
months without starving to death.

At the end of my first month with the Red Cross in
Pusan, President Rhee asked me to join the Government in Taegu and take the directorship of the Office
of Public Information. The director, Dr. Chul-won
Rhee, was broken in health under the strain of war and
needed an indefinite period of rest. Considering it as
being drafted into the war and having pledged to do
anything I could for the country, I accepted. The very
day I took the office I had to issue a statement that the
Government was moving again, this time down to
Pusan. The enemy was near Young-chun, not many
miles from Taegu. The Ministry of Home Affairs was
to stay on in Taegu, for we were not thinking in terms
of evacuating the city. The citizens were requested to
stay by their homes and occupations, keeping everything
as normal as possible. But the road to Pusan was so full
of walking refugees that the line could hardly move
forward. Many of these were refugees from the North
who were by that time accustomed to picking up and
going to the next safety zone.

Arrived back in Pusan after the brief stay in Taegu,
it was necessary to find a lodging place, for the Governor's house was made the temporary residence for
President Rhee and none of us who had previously made
our home there could remain. With refugees in Pusan
taking all available rooms and corners, it was a difficult
thing to find even one room. But with my driver, who

could not stay with Youngyi and me in the same room, we had to have at least two. We were ready to park our jeep and set up an outdoor camp, when a generous host and hostess appeared. They gave their upstairs room to Youngyi and me and let the driver sleep in a corner downstairs. We boarded with them until we could set up our own housekeeping.

Fortunately, in a few weeks the staff at the office found a large, dilapidated old house which they cleaned and repaired enough for us to move in. We called the place "Victory House." But still there was no news of my mother, Chungai, Emma, or any of our other friends still caught in Seoul. Victory House and my heart seemed very empty without them.

As we made the house more livable, many wanted to come and live with us, for it was at a good location. My friend, Maria Pak Lee, with her husband and their two sons came and occupied one section. Defense Minister Syn occupied the upstairs over the Lees. Mr. Hung Soon Lim and some other friends occupied the front part. Youngyi and I had the two rooms in the middle section. Victory House came to be known as a center for refugees from Seoul. As crisis after crisis occurred in the fighting, this house served as a center for information. The occupants sat during sleepless nights breathlessly awaiting what might be the next piece of news.

One day we received word that the enemy were just behind the Masan hills and were expected to occupy Masan within hours. Thereafter nothing could stop their overrunning Pusan. Residents of Pusan were trying to make boat accommodations to pull away to sea in case the Communists entered the city. With clenched fists, members of our staff toured the streets in a bus with a loudspeaker telling the people that we must keep the city. We were trying to convince ourselves as well as others that there was only one course of action left for us.

"Compatriots," we shouted, "where would you go if you left Pusan, the last foothold we have in our fatherland? Is it better to perish at sea as deserters or to die as faithful keepers of a heritage as noble as ours? Stay where you are. The forces from many countries are fighting for us with our soldiers. If we desert our own land, how can we expect others to defend it for us? If we all do our part we will earn our victory together."

A strong UN counteroffensive, launched on August 7 under the direction of General Walton H. Walker, who had succeeded General Dean, stopped the enemy onrush into the area. This turned the tide of that crisis, and the Pusan perimeter was kept intact.

During the latter part of August the battle news began to be in our favor. Our land forces were steadily pushing back the enemy. Secret preparations were under way for some dramatic event, but we did not know what would take place. On September 16 we heard that UN forces under General MacArthur had made an amphibious landing at Inchon on the day before. Recapture of Seoul followed in a few days. Once more it was good to be alive! We were all thinking in terms of return to our capital.

On the twenty-eighth of September we returned to Seoul. All the government officials were notified to assemble at the airport, from which we would leave for the Central Government Building where there was to be a ceremony at nine o'clock.

Over the rubble and ashes we rode through the city of Seoul from the airport and arrived at the bombed and broken building. It was a short ceremony but a dignified one, full of memories of those who had died. In the

130

ceremony General MacArthur graciously handed over the symbol of the city to President Syngman Rhee in the name of the United Nations Command. It was a never-to-be-forgotten scene with the upturned faces speaking more explicitly than words all the things the people had gone through mentally and physically during the three months of communist occupation of Seoul and of most of the South below the thirty-eighth parallel.

As Director of the Office of Public Information, I had to issue the first statement to the citizens concerning the return of the Government to Seoul. It was not an easy task, for so far no statement had been issued as to why and how the Government had left Seoul three months before without informing the people. Some had literally gone through hell, and members of some families had been kidnapped by the Communists. The people were still bitter against "the irresponsible government deserters," as they called them. We of the Office of Public Information felt we must start this first statement with an apology to the citizens of Seoul. Even though what had happened was inevitable, there could have been more information, understanding, and sympathy between the people and the Government. The statement helped some in melting away the bitter feelings.

After my immediate duties were finished, I hurried to the section of town where my mother and friends were staying. Their horrible experiences of hunger, fear, and confinement made them look like different people. The friends I met one after another all looked emaciated. There was no strength, no color, and no spirit left in them. Furthermore, many faces were missing; for they had either been killed or taken as captives to the North by the retreating army. Many of my closest friends, among them Professor Myung Hyuk Lee of our Biology Department, Dr. Joo-sam Ryang of our Methodist church, and Yea-soon Choi of the YWCA, were among the missing. No news has ever come of them.

Our Ewha campus was still off limits, for units of the American Army and Air Force were occupying some of the buildings. Over seventy percent of the city had been destroyed, and our campus had not escaped. The Air Force general told me how sorry he was about our campus. The communist army had occupied it and would not leave during the battle of Seoul. He tried to save the buildings, waiting in the air for the Communists to evacuate the campus. When the Communists set fire to one of the buildings, Pfeiffer Hall, and smoke began to rise out of it, he had ordered the bombs to be dropped, for there was no point in further waiting. Thus we found the campus in ruins, but we rejoiced over the fact that the Communists had been driven out of it.

Although we had returned to Seoul, we were still at war with the Communists. All the United Nations personnel in connection with the Army, agencies for civilian aid, and a countless number of foreign correspondents were with us. How to keep them informed was a big problem. An English daily became an acute need. I consulted President Rhee and proposed that the Office of Public Information start one, since in view of all the destruction no private person or agency could handle it. President Rhee stressed the fact that such a paper should be independent rather than government sponsored. I agreed with this and put the challenge to Mr. Sang Yong Kim, the dean of our university. It was like him to accept the responsibility, and with some other colleagues from Ewha University he started to work at once.

A corporation was organized, some capital gathered, and staff members were assembled. A printing press was the most difficult thing to set up, but it was managed by the skilled labor of the type makers and typesetters. From the Western point of view the press belonged not to the twentieth century but to the sixteenth or seventeenth. Nevertheless the first issue of *The Korea Times* made its debut early in November. More than half of the copies were sent to the battlefront and the other half to civilians behind the lines.

Early in November some of us thought we had better start rehabilitating the University, although our campus was occupied by United Nations forces and there was no immediate prospect of their evacuation. I felt that it was time for me to resign from the Office of Public Information and return to university work. Dr. Chul-won Rhee seemed to have recovered his health and could again assume the responsibilities of the office, so after one hundred days as Director of the Office of Public Information, I resigned.

The battle news was thrilling. Town after town in North Korea was being liberated by our army clear up to the border line between Korea and Manchuria. Suddenly the news of the Chinese hordes coming into the war changed the situation. Even before they came down, some of the allies had criticized the way our forces had gone beyond the thirty-eighth parallel. General MacArthur was recalled because he believed in winning the war by getting after the enemy where and when he could.

I know that at the time there was controversy in America over what General MacArthur should have done and should not have done, but as far as we in Korea were concerned the feeling was strong that he should have been allowed to go ahead into North Korea, and then on as far as he could. After all, the collective action against aggression was winning and was stopped by the recall of General MacArthur. Our Army began to retreat with speed. As the forces of General Walker were pushed farther and farther south, we nicknamed him the "retreating general."

By the middle of December we knew we would have to return to Pusan again. This time everybody in Seoul left, for who would knowingly stay under communist occupation a second time? The roads were crowded with people on foot. It was midwinter, the river was frozen, and snow covered the country. The distance to Pusan was three hundred miles and many perished in the bitter cold. The trains were so crowded with people that many suffocated, and some who climbed to the tops of the trains froze to death.

Two busloads of the Ewha faculty and staff, with their families, went down in an old bus we bought for the purpose. Each person had a small bundle of belongings. As far as the school equipment was concerned, we were stripped and really had nothing much to carry except some of the precious records that had escaped destruction. Chungai could not endure the idea of being caught again in Seoul. She went on the first busload and took my mother with her down to Pusan. After the second busload left, I took off in the old jeep and arrived in Pusan late the next day.

And so we came to Pusan a second time. It was a good thing we had Victory House. Every room was filled with friends, colleagues, and their families. We were hard up in everything, but we had good fellowship all the time. After we got a little settled down we considered what we could do to help our country, for we needed activities

134

to keep up our morale. Because it was the second invasion, people felt more discouraged, and all kinds of rumors were spreading. We saw the need to disseminate correct information among our people. We also felt the need of promoting good relations and mutual understanding between our people and those of the United Nations who had been coming into Korea in increasing numbers.

So we organized The Emergency Citizens League for Information and Friendly Relations. A group of friends who were mostly in educational work, colleagues at the University, and friends in the Army and Navy joined the League. Several Ewha graduates and students helped with the work, too. We had the office open all the time, receiving callers and discussing problems.

Refugees from Seoul came more than any other group. Sometimes we took them up to a high point at night so that they could see for themselves how the boats from many countries had come in and were docked in the bay. They needed to be convinced that vessels of the United Nations were coming in with men and supplies to help with the war. Late at night we would listen for the noise of the caravans of heavy army trucks and tanks going through the city streets to the front lines. These were some of the signs that we, who had no access to the secrets of army movements, could catch as news and use to encourage our people.

Groups of Ewha graduates were organized to visit the fighting units stationed near Pusan with musical programs. Sometimes they gave parties for the soldiers. At these dance parties I had to escort the graduates personally, because their parents would consent only on that condition. These girls did much in helping the foreign personnel to understand and appreciate the Korean people and culture. We had frequent parties at Victory House for the same purpose. Many officers of the Army, Navy, and Air Force, as well as representative civilian personnel, were entertained there. This type of exchange and fellowship became so valuable that we opened similar centers in Taegu and Seoul, choosing the name "United Nations Korean Home." We tried to provide a place where the fighting personnel could, in their spare moments, come in contact with the best of Korean culture in an informal and homey atmosphere. Many came and took advantage of this opportunity.

In addition to these personal contacts the Citizens League issued a bimonthly magazine called *Korea* which introduced our land and people. An attempt was made to present Korean life and culture from an historical perspective. Copies of the magazine were in demand not only in Korea, but also in the countries from which the fighting personnel came. Mr. Chi-tae Kim, a prosperous businessman of Pusan, paid for the cost of six issues. To our sorrow, this project could not be continued for lack of funds.

But *The Korea Times* under the able leadership of Dean Sang Yong Kim continued its daily issues and services to non-Korean-speaking participants in the war, both military and civilian. Early in January, 1951, the whole staff of editors, reporters, and printers came down to Pusan and set up their equipment in dark and crowded quarters temporarily built with wooden boards and tent material. In these inadequate quarters, faced with the daily necessity of providing food for the staff and materials for the press, Mr. Kim carried on the publication for more than a year. During the summer of 1952 he died suddenly. None of us had even suspected that he was sick.

This was a hard blow to all of us, but particularly to *The Korea Times,* which was struggling for existence. Everyone was living from hand to mouth and none of the League members had means to contribute to its support. Having lost its central figure, *The Korea Times* had a very slim chance of being continued. After considering several possibilities, the League wanted to use my name as the editor and publisher. So, assisted by the able staff, I assumed responsibility for the paper. We were able to get a new building of our own, and moved out of the rented and impossible quarters. The business side was getting a little bit better in a year, and the important service was continued.

Also in Victory House the League set up a temporary miniature museum of Korean arts. We realized as we listened to the words of people like General Van Fleet, and others, that the only things the soldiers were experiencing in our country were the terrible battle scenes and storms of dust as they moved back and forth. Our small museum was arranged and opened so that the soldiers could come and see something else pertaining to Korea besides blood and dust. It helped, too, to keep up the morale of our own group in exile.

We were able to assemble a few precious specimens of old pottery and other art objects from people who had brought them when they came as refugees to Pusan. Nobody had a way of making a living, and these treasured objects were being sold at very cheap prices in the market in order to buy provisions. Some were exchanged for cartons of cigarettes or other things that would not begin to compare in value with the antiques, but which could be more easily converted into money. And so priceless objects were going into the hands of foreigners who were not capable of appreciating and preserving them.

Some of us became aware of this situation and began to collect the antiques ourselves. Of course we had no money; but if we skipped a meal, or sold a dress, we could get some of the objects into our own hands.

In all these activities at Victory House, Chungai's contribution was great, especially in the establishment of the museum. Although she was ill with cancer and suffered a great deal of pain, she successfully tried to forget it and do what she could to help from "behind the scenes." She took the responsibility of the management of the big household at Victory House, was in charge of the large and frequent parties for our fighting friends from overseas, and faced the constant need of getting money for increasing expenses. Often she sold her clothes to make ends meet or to purchase some of the precious art objects. Close friends who knew the situation, marveled at her poise and ability, and looked to her for advice and help in time of their own troubles.

Partly to forget her pain, Chungai started caligraphy work and asked us to join her when we had some spare moments. Caligraphy used to be an art to be acquired by all students. It is the study of basic strokes in brush writing. It begins with the writing of Chinese characters, then develops into the painting of the four classic flowers—plum, orchid, chrysanthemum, and bamboo—and on to more complicated objects like birds, animals, and landscapes. Usually the picture is not the target; the whole aim is to interpret a classic poem. After the picture is finished, the poem is copied in the most conspicuous spot. So you can describe caligraphy as the art of interpreting the classics through pictures. In the modernization of our school curriculum, we almost lost

138

this art. So this interest in caligraphy was a significant beginning of the renaissance of our old Korean art amid the chaotic conditions of war and refugee life.

In May 1951, the members of our Citizens League dispatched two representatives to New York to take a message of appreciation to the United Nations and to the permanent delegations of the sixteen countries whose soldiers were taking collective action in Korea—the first such action in history against an aggressor. Mr. Dong-sung Kim and I were sent. We called on the President of the Security Council and the Secretary-General of the United Nations to relay our message. Then one by one we called on the permanent delegates of the sixteen countries. Both at the UN and from the individual delegations we had a cordial reception. We felt it worthwhile to be telling these representatives how grateful our people were for their aid and for the significant action, from a historical perspective, they were taking in Korea for collective security against unprovoked aggression.

Although we were not able to visit the heads of other states, we decided to go to Washington, D. C., and give the message from our people directly to President Truman. The Chaplain of the Senate, Dr. Frederick Brown Harris, secured for us an audience with the President. He seemed very much troubled about the war and repeatedly told us, "It must be a limited war." We said one thing, he said another thing; and neither our minds nor our hearts experienced a meeting point. I think he was so anxious not to have the Korean War spread beyond the thirty-eighth parallel into Manchuria and possibly into China, that he was unable to feel and accept the great surge of emotions and sentiments of gratitude and appreciation that our entire people had for him. However, we still retain these feelings toward him and would like to see him listed among the great presidents of the United States because of his noble and courageous decision to send forces into Korea to check the communist aggression.

In August 1951, we were informed that the time of return to Seoul was indefinitely postponed. On March 15 our forces under the command of General James A. Van Fleet had recaptured the city of Seoul, but no civilians were allowed to return. The faculty and staff of Ewha reviewed the situation and decided to reopen the University in exile. At Victory House a temporary office was opened. We secured the use of a hillside in Pumin Dong near the Provincial Government Building. We began to build up terraces and to erect tents and huts on them for classrooms, laboratories, a library, and small practice rooms, which we called music boxes.

When a sufficient number of tents or huts were ready, nine hundred students reassembled out of about twelve hundred who had been at Ewha at the time of the dispersion in June 1950. Each of us had gone through much distress during the interval, but it seemed at this first meeting that we had never been separated. Some had lost the entire family, some were burdened with the care of young brothers and sisters, some were in rags, some in decent clothes; but we came back to teach and to study again. With sorrow and sadness for the lost ones and with joy and gratitude for the living, on September 1, 1951, we had a grand opening of our college in exile, a most significant event in the history of our institution. We felt that God was in it all. Our voices were choked with emotion as we sang the great hymns of praise and as we prayed for God's blessing upon our new venture.

As time went on we put up more tents, shacks, and

"music boxes." After Seoul was recaptured by our forces, some of the UN army personnel occupied our Ewha campus. There was still some usable material left, such as laboratory equipment, a few books in the library, and six old pianos. These things were transported down to Pusan by the Army, which recognized the importance of keeping up civilian morale and welcomed our efforts to reopen the University. The Army personnel did all they could to help us.

The pianos were put into the music boxes built for that purpose on the top level of terraces. Each music box was big enough for a piano, a student, and a teacher. One of the girls who started her training in one of these boxes, Kyu Soon Lee, is at present a leading chorus director in our College of Music. One of the larger tents served as library. In the winter of 1952 we had an unusually heavy snowfall which broke down the library tent and several others. Some suggested that we dismiss the school until the broken tents were repaired. "Stop college for a little snow?" I exclaimed. "They are temporary buildings, quickly built. They have fallen down quickly; they can be built up again quickly." In no time they were repaired for use and the classes continued.

One tent was designated for our kindergarten, since we carried on the whole program of work that we had had in Seoul. Of course all these tents had dirt floors and the girls sat on them, or on straw mats or pieces of paper on the ground, for chairs were luxuries in those days. The students in Medicine and Nursing needed hospital work. We found a site in the center of the town near the marketplace and built a better and stronger shack-style hospital, adequate under war conditions to give clinical service in all departments.

The last thing we built was our refugee auditorium and chapel on the ground level of the terraces, also in shack-style. This enabled us to come together once every day and kept us united in spirit and in devotion to all that is noble and worthwhile. We restarted our university church services here and had great blessings in Christian fellowship.

After we had accomplished this much, we wanted to have our missionary teachers return. Everybody concerned felt it was a possibility if we could provide living quarters for them. On top of the terraces, ninety-nine steps up, we found a nice site adjoining the college tents and shacks. A wooden structure was put up big enough to accommodate four or five persons. At least, it had a million dollar view of the city and the harbor. Two former Ewha teachers and two new ones came and occupied the house. They were Miss Marion Conrow, Miss Clara Howard, Miss Frances Fulton and Miss Kathleen Crane. Life was rugged but they enjoyed working, and walking up and down the ninety-nine steps!

During the refugee years the clothes of our student body showed a drastic change. Most of the students had come with just one suit of clothes. As spring came on they needed new ones. In the meantime our friends in the United States had been sending relief clothing for them. The group of "Ewha Friends" in Wichita, Kansas, had a sweater campaign for our students and sent one for each girl. Because they had no choice, the girls wore what they had and what they received as gifts. Gradually their clothes all changed to Western style, usually a blouse and skirt or a sweater and skirt, or slacks. This became the custom, and today practically all our students and working girls find it more convenient to wear Western style clothes, reserving their flowing Korean garments for dress-up occasions only.

All around the Pusan perimeter schools were reappearing. The training of more teachers became a desperate need. Using the Kindergarten and the Education Department as a nucleus, we established the College of Education. Student enrollment kept increasing, demanding expansion of the curriculum in other fields. The colleges of Law and Political Science were added. The demand for better prepared teachers and leaders was getting so great that we started the Graduate School. With the added curriculum and the growing student body, we were fast outgrowing the refugee campus, and were relieved when we heard we might return to the Seoul campus in the summer of 1953.

X

THE RETURN TO SEOUL

We had waited longingly for the unification of our country; and in our churches, in prayer groups, and in our individual devotions we had prayed earnestly for it. From the beginning of the Korean War we had thought that with the aid of the UN forces we could drive right on through the North, expel the communist regime and bring about the unification of our country. We had thought that when the Armistice was signed, the UN would hold out for unification. But nothing of that kind happened. On July 27, 1953, the Military Armistice was signed at Pan-mun-jom providing for a cease-fire and establishing a demarcation line between North and South Korea. This was to be a neutral buffer zone along the stabilized battle line. Inspection teams from neutral nations were to insure against violation of the truce.

The dividing line got more formally established and the foreign army personnel guarding the line was increased. That is why we could not accept this armistice nor could we consider it a fair deal to the Korean people who wanted and still want unification.

Still, it was better for everyone to reestablish normal living; and since civilians were allowed to return to Seoul, all during the summer months people were flocking back. Many returned to find their lots piled up with the debris of their former homes. My friend Un-sook Saw, of our Ewha faculty, was one of those who found her house destroyed, except for one room. She considered herself fortunate to have had any part of it spared, and started life again in that one room. Some, after walking the long distance back to Seoul, could not even identify the location where their houses had stood. But still they came.

High school graduates in the Seoul area wanted an opportunity for college work, and requested us to re-open the University even before the entire institution had moved up from Pusan. UN fighting groups had stayed on amid the ruins of our campus for three years. A communications unit occupied the basement and first floor of Pfeiffer Hall, and an airways and air communications service group of the United States Air Force occupied the Music Building. Soldiers lived in the dormitory, and officers in Longview. In January 1953, these occupying units evacuated the buildings and we were able to start a freshman class on the Seoul campus by the first of April. Professor Yong-Jae Kim went to Seoul and managed the work there, while I commuted back and forth between the two campuses.

In Pusan, as soon as summer vacation began, we packed up crate after crate of books, other equipment, and pianos. Once again the army trains facilitated the transportation of our many boxes and crates. By the end of August we had moved back to the ruins of our Seoul campus, full of joy for return and hope for rehabilitation. We immediately started repairs with funds the missions and friends had sent us from abroad, mostly from the United States and Canada.

Through the Cooperating Board of Missions, rehabilitation funds were coming in from the Woman's Division of Christian Service of The Methodist Church in the United States and the Woman's Committee of the Board of Missions of the United Church of Canada. I remember vividly the first personal check for five thousand dollars received for rehabilitation from Mr. and Mrs.

145

Stanley Kresge. These were gifts which bought cement, bricks, and other materials for repairs; but more than that, such expressions of love and concern brought healing to our war-torn wounds which were much deeper than any visible destruction.

By September classes were resumed, although the buildings had no doors or window frames. Fortunately the weather was still warm. Due to the sacrificial devotion and tireless work of our construction staff, the rehabilitation of the partially destroyed buildings was finished in November and all the windows were in before the bitter cold weather. On Thanksgiving Day we had our first general convocation on the athletic field. There was no other place on the campus where over two thousand students and faculty could meet. So we all stood in rows on the field, worshiping God and singing praises for all the wonderful things He had done for us through the past months and years of adversity.

The expansion program which had begun after the Japanese liberation had continued even through the war years, and now that we were back in Seoul it became more accelerated. We had more than two thousand students in September, 1953. Every year there was an increase; but, through a very stiff entrance examination, we kept our freshman class down to one thousand.

The building program which had started prior to the war needed to be reinstated. First of all, Science Hall, which was to be dedicated to the memory of Dr. Alice Appenzeller, had to be finished. She had known before her death that the building was to be named in her honor and was glad. She had never wanted a "cold looking statue" of herself but liked the idea of this building bearing her name, the girls going in and out making of it a living memorial. The building, standing like a twin to Pfeiffer Hall, provided lecture rooms and laboratories for basic sciences, as well as for specialized courses in science for our medical and pharmacy students. Now the campus began to have a New Look.

Next came Wichita House, the President's residence, which was finished and occupied in November, 1955. This house had been conceived and undertaken by the group of "Friends of Ewha" in Wichita, Kansas. The materials had all been stored and the building had been started just before the Korean War broke out. During the war everything was lost, even the basement that had been excavated. We had to start all over again, redrawing the plans to fit the funds left over from the Wichita gift and supplemented by the Woman's Division of Christian Service of the Board of Missions of The Methodist Church in the United States.

Along with this comparatively small building, we were working on an auditorium. We decided to make it big enough to accommodate the whole student body, which now numbered four thousand. As a result it turned out to be the largest auditorium in Korea. Since 1956 would be our seventieth anniversary year, we decided to dedicate this building as our seventieth anniversary memorial. It was to be called the Welch-Ryang Auditorium in honor of Bishop Herbert Welch, who as the first resident bishop in Korea had helped us so much in our first formative years, and Bishop Joo-sam Ryang, who had been our first Korean bishop and the Chairman of our Board of Trustees for several years. He was a victim of the Communists during the first terrible months of the Korean War.

The parents of our students and the Patrons' Association were enthusiastic over our building program and promised to take a big share of the financial responsibility. When the representatives of the Ewha Cooperating Board from the United States—Miss Henrietta Gibson, now the wife of Bishop W. Earl Ledden, Mrs. J. W. Masland, and Mrs. S. E. McCreless—came to the anniversary celebration in May, 1956, agreement was reached for a two-million-dollar building program. The responsibility would be shared equally by the Cooperating Board of the United States and Canada, and the Patrons' Association in Korea. This plan has been working out very effectively ever since, and we are nearing completion of the program.

The building of our steel and concrete auditorium was not an easy thing to handle even after the funds were made available. Skill and materials were both scarce, but all the available experience was placed at our disposal. It was the first building of its kind that our architects had planned, and builders and architects worked on plans and specifications in consultation rather than in competition. Their purpose was to complete a good building. By banding together and pooling all their resources, they were able to plan and build this splendid edifice in time for our Seventieth Anniversary Convocation on May 31. They literally worked until the early morning hours of that day. The final touches to this building are still awaited, for we had to turn to other fundamental needs in the construction program. It is hoped that funds will be provided for its completion to make it a thing of beauty.

A library, more classrooms, and more laboratories were urgent. We had to have a practice kindergarten, and model primary and high schools. Additions to the hospital and the community center all needed their turn. Happy Hall, the student dining room, went up in smoke overnight and still awaits its turn for replacement. Temporarily we moved our dining room into the basement of the auditorium, where the heating plant is waiting for its turn. It is a very gloomy substitute to Happy Hall, but we must wait until another Happy Hall can be built.

We were able to put up a dormitory to accommodate another six hundred girls with funds given largely by the Woman's Division of Christian Service, which Dr. Margaret Billingsley represents in its work in Korea. When Miss Billingsley became Executive Secretary for Korea under the Woman's Division of Christian Service of The Methodist Church, she was not a stranger to us. She had worked in Korea as a missionary and was an old friend. She has given invaluable help in advising with us and in helping secure needed funds and equipment. The new dormitory is called in her honor Billingsley Hall.

There was need of an overbridge which would give us a better entrance and a real gate into the campus. Everything was needed at once; but we set priorities, and building by building our plans were completed. At present a large classroom building, an absolute necessity, is under construction. Still to come are a second gymnasium and a real chapel for worship only. These are items in the ever growing needs of Ewha, which educates more than half the college women of Korea. Monetary gifts and a lot of love and concern and constant prayers of many friends, principally in the United States and Canada, have helped God perform the miracle upon our campus. Those who visit Ewha exclaim, "Simply wonderful! A modern miracle!"

As part of our seventieth anniversary program we scheduled one week in November as Spiritual Emphasis Week. From the beginning years, ever since I can remember, our institution always had a week of revival meetings each year. But under the Japanese occupation and in the confusion of liberation and war, we had been unable to continue this particular annual event. All of us were being deprived by our own negligence of the special opportunity to grow in Christian grace from year to year. The seventieth anniversary was a good year to restore this program for our rehabilitation as persons with souls, along with the rehabilitation of our buildings and equipment.

To lead our meeting we found a man of God and a lover of Korea and its people in the person of Dr. Harry Denman, the General Secretary of the Board of Evangelism of The Methodist Church in the United States. His simple and direct messages won many hearts to Christ and stimulated lukewarm Christians to return to a glowing faith. Hundreds of our students and faculty were led to embrace the Christian faith for the first time or to recommit themselves to Christ and rededicate themselves to follow Him in the service of men.

The second year Dr. J. Manning Potts, Editor of *The Upper Room,* came. Dr. Denman and Dr. Potts returned year after year with teams of outstanding pastors, laymen, and laywomen. Some who came in succeeding years were Mrs. George W. Amos, the Reverend Lee A. Bedford, Mrs. J. A. Berry, Dr. Louise Branscomb, Mr. Jimmy Davis, the Reverend Robert E. Forest, the Reverend Leo K. Gee, the Reverend and Mrs. E. L. Hillman, Mr. Charles Pelzel, the Reverend Reginald H. Potts III, Mrs. R. G. Pullen, Mrs. Milton Randolph, the Reverend Marshall R. Semingson, Mrs. Edward H. Stahly, and Mrs. Robert Wildman. Others are mentioned later.

Literally thousands of our young men and women and

girls and boys have come into contact with the person of Christ. They have been challenged to His way of life and have committed themselves to His cause. We have seen some of these wonders and miracles performed on our campus as well as on other campuses throughout South Korea.

But back to our story. In the fall of 1953, *The Korea Times* had returned to Seoul. It was managed by Mr. Wanbok Choi of our university faculty, under my general supervision, and was getting along nicely when for some unknown reason the Government began to exert constant pressure against it.

In the meantime my strong and able friend Mr. Kiyoung Chang had changed his profession from banking to journalism. He was already making a success in helping *Chosun Ilbo,* one of the oldest daily newspapers, rehabilitate after the war. Upon consultation, he agreed to relieve me of the responsibility of *The Korea Times* and I handed it over to him with two conditions: to keep the independent point of view and to continue daily issues no matter how hard up he might get. Thus I parted with my cherished project in the spring of 1954. Mr. Chang kept up the two conditions and *The Korea Times* is still the only English daily in Korea with an independent point of view.

In the spring of 1953 when we were all preparing to return to Seoul I had had to face the problem of finding a home where I could have my mother and my friend, Chungai, with me. Both had been sick all through our stay in Pusan. There was no place available on or near the campus in Seoul. Then I heard that the family of an Ewha graduate, Yun-kyung Yun, wanted to sell their home to buy in a different location. So we transacted the business immediately there in Pusan and

I bought the Seoul town house. Chungai and I flew up from Pusan and examined the house for the first time. We liked everything about it except the fact that no cars could come to it. But the quaint old Korean gate was too picturesque to change. It was a house of genuine Korean architecture with some modern conveniences. It was a real haven after the refugee life in Pusan. We called it Town House.

In this house Chungai continued her interest in caligraphy as long as she could sit up. Her interest in collecting old art objects also continued. The major part of her collection consisted of Koryu and Li dynasty pottery. The grayish green glaze of Koryu celadon and the milk-white and blue beauties of the Li period were most cherished by her. The Ewha collection had all been lost in the war, and Chungai's collection became the nucleus of the miniature museum in Pusan which was newly set up at Ewha University. So she continued collecting art objects through the autumn months. From the winter months she was in great pain and spent most of her time in bed. Great numbers of friends were always with her at home as her illness grew worse and worse.

As for my mother, she had wanted to return to her own room on the campus but this had been destroyed in the war and we could not replace it. Mrs. Kim, my mother's adopted daughter and the mother of my friend and colleague, Okgill, had taken care of mother after Chungai became so sick in Pusan. Mrs. Kim's refugee home was in Suyong near Pusan. Here mother had been bedfast for some months, with her mind not clear at times. She was nearing ninety years of age. We had to wait until October to bring her to Seoul until her own room on Mrs. Kim's grounds could be finished, since Mrs. Kim wanted to continue to take care of mother to relieve me from the responsibility of two patients who both needed constant vigil and care.

In the late fall and early winter mother seemed to get a little better, but in February the tide turned and she was in a coma most of the time. One morning when she came to herself, Mrs. Kim and I took her to our Town House where we wanted her to spend her last days. She knew what was happening to her and liked it. Her consciousness remained clear for some time. I asked, "Mother, do you know where you are?" She smiled and answered, "Yes, I am where I ought to be." She grew weaker and weaker and finally left us on February 13, 1954.

Relatives, friends, and colleagues helped with her funeral. Services were held in her own Chung Dong church which was full to overflowing, and the funeral procession was as long as she would have wanted it to be, and even longer. She had always told me she wanted "a grand funeral," and I was happy I could fulfill this last wish of hers. Her burial ground was on the top of a mountain overlooking the Han river at Mang-Wu-Rie. Many who were present at her funeral said, "She couldn't have chosen a more beautiful spot if she had taken all her life to look for it."

During her lifetime, everywhere mother went she established a church if there was none. There had been no church in the new neighborhood where she lived during her last years. Now a small church stands there in her memory.

Meanwhile, Chungai's illness became more and more serious. She went to bed early in February and never got up again. She endured the pain and did not take sedatives until the very last. Many friends who came to see her left after their visit smiling and cheerful. One of her young friends, Okgill's brother Dongill Arthur Kim, helped her to prepare for her homegoing. She loved his singing and his weekly visits were a comfort to her. Toward the end he came oftener to sing. For her physical needs she depended upon Okgill, and upon Lucy, who had been our housekeeper for many years.

Two days before her death she was in a happy mood and told me that she would follow me everywhere. Leaving me was the last care that bothered her, but she told me she had committed even that into God's hands, and she was at perfect peace of mind and heart. "We will just say good night when you go to sleep first," I said, "then we will say good morning when we both wake up over there." She fell asleep on May 9, 1954, in such beauty and peace that it was a blessed experience for some of us who were privileged to watch. We all bowed our heads after her last breath and offered a prayer of thanks for her life and for the victory over death that her faith in Christ made possible.

Chungai had wished to be cremated and her ashes scattered to the four winds, but her mother begged that her ashes be buried in a spot which would be sacred to her memory. Through the winter months an idea of developing a beautiful memorial garden had come to me. Her family and friends all approved.

In the spring of 1955 we purchased a small plot of land where there was not a single blade of grass, and moved her ashes to a sunny spot. Then we began to plant trees and shrubbery. During the years little by little it has become a beautiful place with trees, grass, flowers, fruit orchard, and even some goldfish in the pond. We call it Friendship Garden and a group of friends make weekly visits on Sunday afternoons for rest and fellowship. It is about ten miles from Ewha, near enough for frequent visits. All the year round the garden adorns itself in the different charms of the seasons. When it is covered with snow its beauty is just as breathtaking as when it is clothed in all the glories of spring flowers. Among the friends who gather there is Arthur Kim, now a professor at Yonsei University in Seoul. His lovely voice so often comforted Chungai during her illness, and now often he sings for us in Friendship Garden. Across a hill we can see the cemetery where our dear friend, Maria Pak Lee, and her family were buried following their tragic deaths during the uprising of April, 1960.

With mother and Chungai gone, I thought at first I was going to be quite alone. I was wrong in thinking so. My friends surround me with tender care and happy companionship beyond my deserving. Not only at home but even when I am abroad, in most of the cities to which my travels carry me, I find a group of friends and graduates of Ewha who make me feel at home. I have many homes all over the world filled with families not born of the flesh but of the spirit and of love.

Several activities that Chungai started at Town House still continue. One of them is the caligraphy class. About fifteen members meet together on the last Saturday of each month to study brush writing and painting. Some bring their work to be criticized by the teachers and to receive new assignments. But the most interesting part of the whole afternoon and evening program is to watch our teachers write and paint for us. They use the pen names Young-Woon, Woo-Chung, E-dang, Song-sun, Chung-jun, and Kong-jung. Every year we prepare an exhibition to commemorate the ninth of May, the anniversary of Chungai's death. My own participation in this class has been very discouraging because lack of time makes it impossible for me to keep up my practice. Instead of making progress I go backward. But my great interest in it will continue through the years ahead.

The museum at Ewha is a constant reminder of Chungai's interest in collecting and preserving Korean antiques. It is now housed in a beautiful building and is considered the best museum of any university in Korea.

Under the Japanese regime we were invaded not only geographically and politically, but culturally. Our way of life and our language were almost forbidden, and from the time I was very small there was no history of our own in our curriculum. We grew up as a generation hungry for knowledge about our own history and culture. So while we were still under the Japanese regime, through the Home Economics Department we started to collect old objects pertaining to everyday life in the home. This was the pretext under which we could begin the collection without arousing too much suspicion of nationalism. We had quite a collection of cooking utensils, dishes, clothes, ornaments that women used to wear in the olden days, and all kinds of household objects. Our collection was considered excellent, and we were proud of it.

In 1950, when the Communists took over Seoul, one of the first things they confiscated was our museum. When we were permitted to return to Seoul, we brought back from Pusan quite a collection of small but precious antique pieces. They were small because people had not been able to carry large pieces into exile. Seoul was in ruins, and even after our return people were continuing to sell their heirlooms in exchange for provisions. Also, in the antique shops of Seoul there were some very precious pieces, and the prices were

156

quite cheap. As we had done in Pusan, Chungai and I, as well as others, bought as many of these pieces as we could.

From that time on the collection has grown and now contains artifacts from the earliest periods of Korean culture. The earliest recorded history of Korea begins with 57 B.C.; but the legendary roots of our history extend back beyond 2000 B.C., or to the Stone Age of Korean culture. Artifacts from this period include stone axes, and stones for grinding and for making fire.

The earliest extant Korean pottery dates from the Silla period (57 B.C.-A.D. 936). From this period our museum has earthen vessels of exquisite form and decoration. These are hand molded and decorated with incised patterns. Most of this ware is unglazed, although there are specimens of glazed ware belonging to the late Silla period.

The museum contains quite a collection of the world-famous glazed celadon ware of the Koryu Period (A.D. 936-1392). The decorations are etched or engraved in the body of the ware with a knife or pointed tool. Some later pieces show the incised designs inlaid with black and white clays. The best specimens, which belong to the period between 1050 and 1170, are the bluish green celadon. In addition to the soft bluish green ware, some pieces are brownish or grayish in color.

The Li period (1392-1910) is noted for its painted ware with distinctive translucent glaze. In our museum are some particularly beautiful blue and white combinations. Also from the Li period we have silver and gold ornaments from the tombs of the royal families, and several rare scrolls.

At the time of the completion of the arts building, Mr. Hyung Koo Sim was the curator of the museum.

In 1962 he was accidentally drowned while swimming in the sea. His death was a great loss to Ewha where, in addition to his duties as curator of the museum, he had served as a professor of art and as dean of the College of Music and Fine Arts. His wife is a talented musician with a lovely operatic soprano voice.

Mr. Sim was an artist in his own right. He had studied art at Columbia University and at the Art Student League in New York. Private showings of his oil paintings were held in Seoul and his paintings were twice honored in the Japan Imperial Exhibition. From 1947 to 1958 he was a visiting professor in the Art Department of Adelphi College in New York.

While Mr. Sim was curator of the museum at Ewha, an exchange of art objects was arranged with The Upper Room Museum in Nashville, Tennessee. The Korean exhibit in The Upper Room Museum is a memorial to him.

All these things bring back to us the cultural environment and the artistic taste of our ancestors, and we dream for our future. I have always entertained the idea that if the Korean people have a world contribution to make, it is going to be a cultural contribution. I do not know that we will ever develop, and I do not know that we want to develop, as a military nation; or that we will ever realize great achievements in the world of science. I do not want to limit the future possibilities of our people, but it seems to me that our greatest potential contribution to the world is in the field of the arts.

XI

INTERNATIONAL WINDOWS

Every contact I have had with a person of another nationality has served as an international window. Through that person I could see and sense so much of the culture of his nation. I was fortunate to have had these contacts from my early days in school in the persons of missionary teachers. In later years international friendships were found at Ewha and in many countries under different circumstances. They kept increasing in the number of persons and nationalities; I can mention only a few.

As soon as liberation took place and our country was opened up again, Ewha was frequently visited by outstanding people from all over the world. The visits of great personages such as Marian Anderson and Pearl Buck were high moments on the campus.

We also had noted visitors like the Moderator of the United Church of Canada and the Moderators of the Presbyterian Church from the United States. They said that they were greatly inspired by the students, but I know that it was our students who received the special inspiration from their presence and their messages.

I have already named many international religious leaders who came to Ewha. Another was Dr. Henry P. Van Deusen who visited us before the Second World War, during Dr. Appenzeller's regime. I recall helping show him around the campus. In later years when I knew him more personally through the meetings of the International Missionary Council, he always spoke with encouragement of our work at Ewha. I have wished he could come again and see our campus of the present time. Spirits like his, I am proud to say, seem to have met with spirits akin to his when he visited us; and he seems to understand us.

When the United Nations Temporary Commission on Korea began its work in 1948, persons of different nationalities came in as members of the Commission and its staff. The first chairman was Mr. K. P. S. Menon from India. Throughout our history we have respected and held in high esteem his ancient and great nation. We have also felt a deep understanding and a sympathetic kinship of suffering, since our two countries have both been under alien rule. We expected Mr. Menon to understand our problems and to work only in the best interests of our nation and people.

He proved that he was everything we expected and more. He appreciated our way of life and understood the deep craving in the hearts of the people for national independence and reunification. He worked hard for us until, on the recommendation of the Commission, the Interim Committee of the UN General Assembly decided to carry on general elections throughout Korea in the area accessible. This gave us the birth of our nation as the Republic of Korea. For some reason Mr. Menon's government recalled him and we have never seen him since, although he promised when he left that he would return to see the inauguration of our Republic on August 15, 1948. However, our strong friendship, personal and national, will remain always; and history will record that through him India has made a notable contribution to the development of our nation at its critical point.

Soon after we went down to Pusan the second time, a new administrative secretary arrived for the UN Commission in Korea. He was Mr. George J. Mathieu, a true Frenchman but thoroughly international in his thoughts and actions. He became our friend in no time and we knew that the Korean personnel in the employ of the Commission were being treated fairly, and without discrimination.

Mrs. Mathieu was especially fond of *kimchee,* our fermented fresh vegetable dish. We think *kimchee* is a national dish so unique that when foreigners learn to like it, we tell them they have become Koreans and that they qualify for naturalization. Mrs. Mathieu qualified very readily. Besides, she is Irish, and we Koreans have been called the Irish of the Orient. So the couple have become permanent friends of mine and of Korea, making available to us their opinions and points of view. This is stimulating to our minds, which have the tendency to be highly nationalistic.

While in Pusan, our exile campus on the hillside stood as a symbol of our constructive efforts to do what we could in spite of the war situation. We began to be noted in this respect and therefore were accepted as friends by the commanding generals of the Army and Air Force, and by the admirals of the Navy. I cannot name them all, but they almost always called on us when in Pusan, giving us good fellowship and encouragement. We on our part felt like "buddies" to them and their men. Although we could not share the actual fighting in the front lines, we were determined to do everything possible to help win the war by keeping up morale behind the lines. When changes took place in the personnel of the commanders, which happened often, we suffered the pangs of the separation of real "buddies" on the battlefield.

One of the big group of friends we made during the

war years was General James A. Van Fleet. He and his staff were always our welcome guests at Victory House and at the other UN Korean Homes in Taegu and Seoul. They had helped so much in the moving of our university back and forth between Pusan and Seoul. When Mrs. Van Fleet joined the General in Korea after their only son was missing in action, we wept with them. Another friend was Admiral George C. Dyer who commanded the Seventh Fleet in our waters. We looked forward to his coming with his staff to Victory House and had many good times of fellowship. We were sad to see him leave, but the friendship continued and he and Mrs. Dyer sent us their whole library after we moved the University back to Seoul. Many others in the Air Force became our personal friends, mostly through the UN Korean Home in Taegu where the Air Force headquarters were. Some of the foreign correspondents and newspaper reporters, too, remain friends until today.

International organizations and gatherings on regional or world levels also have opened up great vistas of human relationships and cultural interchange. They always helped to deepen my understanding of men and to widen the horizon of my appreciation for the differences as well as the similarities that exist between lands and peoples, and I hope in turn I have been able to help others understand my country and its people.

The international gatherings I have been privileged to attend have covered a wide range of interests and concerns. Beginning with the Student Christian Conference in 1922, I have attended forty-five such conferences or group meetings on all continents except Australia. Twenty-two were connected with Christian organizations, fourteen were in the area of socio-political concerns, six had to do with women's organizations, and three were in the interests of education in general and of Ewha University in particular.

In addition to these general remarks, I must cite a few specific experiences I have encountered at some of these gatherings which served as even larger windows through which I could see the international problems.

The most exciting experience I had was at the Paris Assembly of the United Nations in 1948. Our Republic had just been inaugurated in August. Again, after thirty-eight years, we were people of an independent nation. Our dreams were many and our hopes high for the new Republic. One of these ambitions was to be recognized as a nation by the UN. As an observer delegation, a group headed by Dr. John M. Chang was appointed and dispatched to Paris in September. Miss Yunsook Moh and I were the only women in the delegation. Most of our work had to be done unofficially behind the scenes, for we had no official status on the floor of any meetings. We had thought it would be an easy thing to secure recognition from the UN since it had been responsible for the creation of the Republic of Korea. "The UN cannot say no to its own baby," was what we said.

As we contacted different delegations, we woke up from our dreams. Opposition from the communist countries was expected from the beginning, but the so-called neutral nations surprised and shocked us as they spoke one after another. Their arguments usually followed two lines of thought. The first was, how could they recognize only South Korea? It would be a most unfair action for an international organization to take. The second was that if the government in South Korea alone were recognized, it would be making permanent the division of the country, which certainly no one wanted.

These were indeed plausible arguments, and a divided Germany provided a similar argument. But there could be no unification of either Korea or Germany until the differences between the free world and the communist were resolved. What were we, the afflicted Korean people, to do in the meantime? We argued and pleaded with every delegation that our new nation be recognized and given a chance to grow and develop into maturity and strength to defend itself as well as to participate in the struggles of the divided world.

Our efforts continued through the months of October and November. By this time we knew who stood with us and how many votes we could depend upon. The friendly powers, led by the Australian, Chinese, and United States delegations, introduced a resolution on December 7 for our recognition, and the Political Committee began its discussions. As expected, the resolution encountered bitter opposition from the Soviet bloc and from some neutral countries. But after many sessions and speeches from both sides, the resolution passed in the Committee by a great majority.

This was indeed the most exciting moment in my life. The next minute I was simply stunned by the silence of our delegation, which rose from the meeting without any expression of thanks or joy in response to the Committee action. Our chief delegate, Dr. Chang, would have it this way, although some of us wanted to shout for happiness and gratitude. I could not decide which was harder to endure at this meeting—listening to the savage words of the Soviet representatives against us or keeping our mouths shut when we felt like shouting *Mansei* after our recognition was voted through.

The last step still remained—the passage of the resolution through the General Assembly. Other urgent matters needed the Assembly's attention. It was on the last day, December 12, and at the last evening session that the resolution for our recognition came up for discussion and vote. Some delegations were already beginning to leave, and many had planned to depart during that evening. We went from one to the other of the friendly delegations urging them to remain until the vote was taken. Each vote in our favor was precious, for it seemed that none of the opposing delegations were leaving.

The midnight hour was fast approaching and still the voting remained to be done. We of the Korean delegation held our breath from minute to minute. After the last speech was finished, voting began and the resolution for our recognition received an overwhelming majority. The members of our delegation felt that we had to do something to celebrate the occasion. We walked the streets shouting and hugging each other. Our chief delegate took us to my first and only night club. The occasion seemed to call for a special celebration, but we could not behave too differently from our accustomed ways all of a sudden. Miss Moh and I watched the show for a while and then went back to our hotel room.

For four successive years, from 1956 to 1959, I was a member of the Korean delegation to the UN General Assembly in New York City. Every year I went for three or four weeks, for that was all I could spare from my university work. Although the Republic of South Korea had been recognized by the UN as an independent nation, we were still an observer delegation. Our work consisted largely of unofficial contacts, made individually or in groups.

I always took an apartment and set it up for temporary housekeeping. Day after day for tea or dinner we invited UN delegates to meet with us. I wanted my apartment to serve as an island of Korea in the big sea of Western civilization. I served special Korean dishes and delicacies. This helped greatly to concentrate our thinking and talking on Korean culture and Korean problems. Ewha graduates in and around New York City let their own work suffer at times to come and help me entertain my guests from many countries. I simply could not have done my work without their assistance.

Attendance at the committee meetings and general sessions of the UN was secondary, but necessary in order to keep up intelligent conversations on the current events at the UN building. There were other social events to attend when the time was available.

One night the delegates from Nepal and our group were having dinner and an entertainment together. Our guests remarked, "It is just like being at home. There is such a great deal of similarity between our two cultures. The food, the dances, and the songs all make us homesick. Someday we want to come and see you and your country." Another group of friends, mostly from the United Kingdom and the United States delegations, left remarks in my book such as these: "I would adore to visit your beautiful Korea," "A glimpse of another life of a very friendly people," "A delightful reunion of old friends, charming new friends, and delicious Korean food."

On one occasion we had a press group for luncheon in our apartment representing sixty to seventy million readers. They were from United Press International, Associated Press, *New York Times, Christian Science Monitor, Newsweek, Reader's Digest, Look, New York Herald Tribune,* and others. Over the Korean dishes, intellectual flashes went back and forth thick and fast on subjects pertaining to Korea, from food to education

166

and international politics. Many of the group said they were having their first Korean meal and liking it tremendously. They looked at the few paintings we had, admired our Korean costumes and were impressed by the pictures of Ewha Womans University. As they left, they all expressed appreciation for this glimpse of Korean culture. To me the intellectual feast of that occasion was of great significance.

All through the spring and summer months of 1958 there was a movement to get ten million signatures of our people to request Korean membership in the UN. Both in Seoul and in the provinces, members of our UN Association sat on street corners and got the signatures of passersby. In October, I joined our UN delegation and presented these ten million signatures.

Every year about the same process takes place at the General Assembly in regard to our membership. The friendly nations present a resolution reconfirming the UN aim in Korea—to establish and rehabilitate a united and independent Korea—and proposing to put the report of the UN Commission on Korea on the agenda of the following year. Then the communist and some neutral nations make statements of opposition to the resolution and the free world countries give speeches supporting it. Finally the resolution is put to the vote and adopted by the majority. That is as far as it goes.

This year our people wanted to strengthen their request for regular UN membership with their own signatures. The big bundles of signatures, about two feet high and four feet long, were too large to carry, so our delegation took one big sample book of the signatures to the Secretary-General, Dag Hammarskjold. He accepted it graciously with sympathy and understanding, but his genial smile was coupled with a telling silence. The reporters who were present took notice of the impressive pile of signatures. That was as far as the signatures went.

To Koreans it is a repeated bitter experience to be kept out of UN membership. From a world point of view, the denial of membership to the Republic of Korea is not half as serious as the fact that this world organization upon which the issue of world peace depends so much cannot at all times implement the mind and will of the majority.

In the summer of 1956 I had a very amazing and perplexing experience in Geneva with the International Committee of the Red Cross. At the time, I was vice-president of the Korean Red Cross, but did not know what was going on in the International Committee. Suddenly in June an urgent request was made that, since I was to be in Europe for other meetings, I go to Geneva. Representing the Korean Red Cross, I was to urge the International Committee of Red Cross not to endorse and assist the plan of the Japanese Red Cross to send Korean residents in Japan to North Korea. Representatives of the Japanese Red Cross and of North Korea were already in Geneva trying to make definite arrangements for the help of the International Committee of the Red Cross. Representing the government of the Republic of Korea, Minister Yong Sik Kim, who was stationed in Geneva, and Minister Kyuha Choi, from the Tokyo mission, were there working on the problem; but no one was present from the Korean Red Cross.

The Committee graciously listened to our explanations and pleas. We requested the Committee not to assist the Japanese Red Cross in the deportation of Korean residents in Japan to North Korea. Mr. Kim, Mr. Choi, and I did our best to explain the historical background of the Korean residents in Japan, and that they were now a burden that the Japanese would like to get rid of. We also tried to tell how the Korean Communists in Japan, under the direction of North Korea, were carrying on false propaganda to mislead the residents. We tried to point out that the willingness of the residents to go to North Korea could not be their true desire but that they had been either bribed or coerced. We said that we certainly thought that the International Red Cross, as a neutral body, would not wish to give assistance to a plan of taking people from the free world for labor behind the iron curtain. We added that the Korean Red Cross and the entire people and government of Korea begged them to keep their hands off such a scheme; that we could not tolerate the deportation of so many of our compatriots to the slavery of the communist world.

The International Committee of the Red Cross in turn tried to help us understand its historical background; its structure and operations; its finances; and, most of all, its unchangeable and immovable position of neutrality, with readiness to render service whenever a human need becomes imperative. The Committee maintained that in this case its service would be to meet the needs of a great mass of people wanting to go to North Korea to reside, and to be on hand to ascertain that no one would be sent against his will.

The more we tried to talk with each other the farther apart we seemed from one another. Our minds were working as unrelated machines, our emotional leanings faced opposite directions, and the very grounds we each stood upon were two different worlds. The members of the Committee spoke a Swiss tongue, we spoke Korean and never the two could understand each other. I found that the reasoning of the Neutrals was just as difficult to understand as that of the Communists, and more disappointing; for, naively, I had expected understanding from the former. Finally the International Committee of the Red Cross decided to help Japan deport thousands of Koreans to North Korea.

To date the number has reached seventy-five thousand or more. As far as I know this is the only mass migration from the free world to behind the iron curtain. To the Red Cross this may be considered as a worthy achievement, but to us in South Korea it will remain, to say the least, a questionable decision. What will be the answer, not a practical but a moral one, when thousands of Korean children deported with their parents some day raise the question, "Why were we deprived of the chance to grow and live in the free world?"

In 1955 the Asian Peoples Anti-Communist League was conceived and born in Korea. I think this is the first and only international organization founded in Korea so far. The purpose of it is evident in its name. It has grown steadily during the years and at the Extraordinary Conference held in Korea in May, 1962, representatives from sixteen member and fifteen observer nations, and four fraternal units met together. The most significant action taken at that time was to establish a Freedom Center in Korea. The purpose of the Center is to carry on research on communism and how to combat it, and to train leaders to prevent its spread and to meet it effectively wherever it appears in any of its phases and stages.

I believe the people in the free world are not entirely aware of the deadly character of communism. If they were, there would already be in the world today many research centers for prevention and cure of this cancerous disease. The Freedom Center in Korea should serve at least as the beginning of a movement to restore the health of humanity from its deadly pestilence of communism. People usually do not wish to enlist their interest in a movement to oppose something, and I share this unwillingness. But in this anticommunist movement I want to be in the forefront, as I would wish to be in any movement to keep our people from catching deadly germs. This is our obligation to all those who have already given their lives to make ours safe. We have seen and heard communism in action. If any nation in the free world knows what it is like, it is Korea; and therefore we have a mission to tell the uninformed or misinformed peoples of the world.

My participation in so many Christian conferences and organizations has opened up the whole world—past, present and future—for fellowship and inspiration. To know the great world personages in Christendom and saintly men and women all around the world who follow Christ in daily devotion and service has been such a rare privilege that I feel unworthy, and yet proud. I cannot begin to name them all, for they make up a great company. The mountaintop experiences at Jerusalem in 1928, at Accra in 1957-1958, and at New Delhi in 1961 carried me up high enough to make possible some projection into the unknown future life. At least I could think, "If Christian fellowship can mean this much while in the flesh, how much more will it mean in the beyond where my spirit will not be bound by the limitations of the body?"

Besides the YWCA and women's missionary conferences, I attended the first Pan-Pacific Women's Conference and the World Congress of the International Federation of University Women. There is such a thing as the Women's World, and it is easily discovered at meetings like these. I always felt perfectly at home enjoying the intimate and informal relationships that one can have at these conferences. It always gave me a great delight and strength to meet and confer with the wonderful women leaders from all over the world.

I often thought how much better the world could be made if many of these able women leaders were in positions of world leadership instead of limiting their activities to their national organizations only. I could almost say with surety that the world would become in a short time more orderly, more constructive, and more peaceful if these women ran it at least half-and-half with equally able and great men.

I have discovered, by and large, great potential in the Western women leaders I have come in contact with; and I have always thought it a shame that their leadership is not sought and used more in positions of great responsibility in all the different phases of their national life, as well as in the ever increasing number of international organizations.

XII

TWO REVOLUTIONS

At six o'clock on the evening of April 19, 1960, about thirty of us were meeting in the garden of Wichita House, the President's residence on the Ewha campus, to organize the Friendship Evangelistic Association. We were people of one mind, most of us from the university church. However, there were friends from other churches, making our Association interdenominational. Just as we were about to begin our supper we heard the crackling of rifle fire in the city. News came that marshal law had been declared and that every citizen should be in his home by seven o'clock. Some of our group had to leave before supper. We always say that our Association was born in revolution.

From the latter part of March, 1960, discontent and tension among the people had been mounting against the Liberal party and the government headed by Dr. Syngman Rhee. When Dr. Rhee had returned from Honolulu in October, 1945, all the leaders and the entire people welcomed him as a national hero and leader unparalleled in history. Subsequently he was elected chairman of the first National Assembly which drew up the Constitution. Then again he was unanimously elected president of our new republic, which was the first independent, democratic form of government in Korea. He had the entire country and the whole populace on his side. Even the leaders of the different political groups, including the leftists, were willing to accept him as the national leader. The people stood solidly behind him, supporting his attitude of noncompromise with the Communists. The confidence of the people in his leadership was almost absolute.

On August 15, 1948, with the inauguration of the Republic of Korea, the list of President Rhee's first cabinet was announced. For the first time some thinking people were surprised, for in their judgment there were people on the list who were chosen for reasons other than their qualifications and the best interests of the nation. But the public in general acquiesced and began to watch. In the following years the tragic weakness of Syngman Rhee—his inability to use the right people in the right places—led his long administration into corruption and eventual downfall in spite of his continued patriotism and devotion to the national welfare. To this day his integrity and patriotism are not questioned, and he is held in high esteem and loved by the people at large.

During the second term of his presidency a constitutional provision was adopted making it possible for him to run for president the third time and to continue to run for the office as long as he lived. This was the beginning of his breach of the Constitution he helped to make. He and some of his party members gradually fell into the damnable habit of interpreting or changing the law to accommodate their political conveniences.

This all helped the growth of a strong opposition, and by the time of Syngman Rhee's third election in 1956, his running mate for the vice-presidency, Mr. Ki-poong Lee, was beaten by Dr. John M. Chang, the candidate of the opposition party. The pro-administration party was called Liberal and the opposition, Democratic. The fight for the vice-presidency was considered to be of great importance since Dr. Rhee was already more than eighty years old. If anything should happen

174

to him, according to our constitution the vice-president would fill out his term of office. So it was just like electing the next president, and the fight had been fierce.

With the arrival of the year 1960, we looked forward to our fourth presidential election. The Liberals had no other thought than to have Dr. Rhee and Mr. Lee run again. The Democrats had Dr. Pyung-ok Chough and Dr. John M. Chang as their candidates. Although Dr. Rhee was getting on in years, he still had good health and an active mind. People in general still considered him the man of the hour. There seemed no other prospect but his election to the presidency again. But a great many people worried over the poor health of Mr. Ki-poong Lee which would make his assistance to the old President not so dependable. An old President and a sick Vice-President would certainly make the outlook for the future gloomy.

While nonpolitical circles worried thus, to the political world it became a grave issue. The Democrats were sure of their chance since they had won in electing the vice-president before. Their presidential candidate, Dr. Chough, died within a few days of election. The vice-presidency was more important anyway, so they concentrated on the campaign for their vice-presidential candidate. On the other hand, the Liberals with their experience of defeat four years before could not rest at ease. The poor health of Mr. Ki-poong Lee would lessen even more his chance over against that of his opponent.

The key men of the Liberal party and those in high government positions began to devise ways and means to increase the votes for the election of Mr. Lee. Irregularities in voting were practiced throughout the country. The Minister of Internal Affairs and the Chief of Police took it upon themselves to get Mr. Lee elected by a big majority. The election announcement was a great surprise to all, for the percentage was over seventy for Mr. Lee. No one but the Minister and the Police Chief knew just how this had happened. I am certain that Dr. Rhee does not know even today, for all the news of the trials was kept from him. However, the election was declared valid.

To the great surprise of the blindfolded leaders, people rose up. The flagrant rigging and dishonesty exercised in the election were known to many who had been deprived of their voting privileges without any reason. And many had been forced to play certain parts in the irregularities. These facts were carried from mouth to mouth. Demonstrations broke loose first in Masan and Taegu, then spread to Seoul.

Once again, as in 1919, the demonstrators were mostly students. They declared the March election invalid and demanded a new and clean one. The police met these demonstrations with force, firing on the students and arresting many. This type of police encounter in Masan infuriated the students of the whole country. One of the reports was that the student leader, Choo-il Kim, was killed and put into the sea to hide from the public the brutality of the police. When the students from Korea University were carrying on demonstrations in Seoul, the police used gangsters and hoodlums to attack and disperse them. This inflamed the populace the more, and the streets of Seoul were filled with students and other demonstrators until no control of any kind could be effective. Students proceeded to President Rhee's residence. On the way some of them were shot down by the police. They persisted in their push until their representatives were let into the residence and saw the President face to face.

It was told by an eyewitness that the student representatives were welcomed by President Rhee. As the President and the students shook hands, both parties wept and were able to talk without any feeling of barrier between them. The students later characterized the President as a great patriot. At their request, and on the advice of others, President Rhee agreed to give up the presidency.

He decided to leave the presidential mansion the next day. "I will go from here to my house," he said. "I am glad that the Korean people are alert and still willing to fight for their freedom. If on my way some people would kill me out of their hatred for the wrongs my administration has committed, I will be only too glad to die at their hands." Instead, the crowds stood in silence and watched his car pass by, some in tears and some in bewilderment.

When the news spread throughout the country, people mourned the loss of their great leader. Some weeks later the Rhees agreed with the authorities that it would be best for them to leave Seoul, and they went into exile in Hawaii. We hear that Dr. Rhee is pining away his last days wanting to come back to his homeland to die.

While the students and the President were inside reaching an understanding and a course of action best for the country, the police were still firing on the crowd which was growing larger and larger outside the presidential mansion. This further infuriated the people. The nearby streets were filling up and the crowds were getting beyond control every minute. Marshal law was quickly declared. In all the major cities mobs were moving around setting fire to buildings, both public and private, and demanding the lives of the unfaithful

177

and disloyal. Police stations, the homes of Liberal party members, and those of other questionable citizens were looted and set on fire.

This happened to the home of Mr. and Mrs. Ki-poong Lee. They were in hiding and no one knew of their whereabouts, but most of the people thought they had safely escaped the hands of the mob. Then early in the morning of April 26, the news of their tragic death reached us. No one really saw what took place. But putting stories together we learned later that after trying to find a place of refuge, the whole family of four met in one of the small houses on the grounds of the presidential mansion. The President's resignation was to become effective and he would leave the grounds on April 27. That would mean no protection for the Lees any longer, and the demonstrators were still searching for them and demanding their lives.

There were only two alternatives left for them, either to throw themselves upon the mercy of the mob or to take their own lives. They chose the latter course. From the description of the scene it appeared that the older son, who was in military service, shot the father, the mother, and the younger brother, and then turned the pistol upon himself. The news of this tragedy spread like an electric shock among the people.

Mrs. Lee (Maria Pak Lee) had been my colleague at the University, in the YWCA and other women's organizations, and in all our church activities. She was our Vice-President in whose charge I had left Ewha whenever I went away on national or church errands. Her family had become dear to us also. Except in her political involvements through her husband and in her friendship with Madame Rhee, we shared our lives and experiences in intimate fellowship from day to day.

When the news of her death reached us, we wished in vain we could have helped her in time. There was something we could and should do yet—arrange for her a decent funeral service and burial. We took the initiative; and under the ministry of our university chaplain, funeral and interment services were held for the entire family. At our first chapel service at the University after the recess, we held a memorial service for our Vice-President, Maria Pak Lee, who had been a respected colleague and dear friend to the faculty, and an inspiring teacher and guide to the students.

In a few days Mr. Chung Huh became head of the Interim Government. He was an experienced administrator with a level head, practical sense, and a conscience governed by principles. The Democratic party, which had been the opposition party for a long time, was now in the limelight. It got a majority in the election of the National Assembly and Mr. Posun Yun was President and Dr. John Myun Chang, Prime Minister. Everything went along nicely until there was a split in the majority party, creating political confusion and instability.

By this time the better elements among the students had gone back to their classes; but all kinds of demonstrations by various and sundry groups continued to take place, compounding the confusion. Society in general deteriorated. Taking advantage of such a situation, the Communists increased their infiltration into the South until the government seemed to be losing its control over its direction and its destiny. People in general began to feel insecure, not knowing what might happen the next minute. Inefficiency and corruption were evident everywhere as the main characteristics of the new government. Everyone who seemed to know anything about politics said, "This government cannot last a year."

In less than a year, on May 16, 1961, the Second Republic of Korea came to an end. The military leaders initiated a coup, having labeled the regime inefficient and corrupt, totally incapable of handling the situation which in time could push the nation into the snares of the Communists. There were already signs of that very thing happening in our midst.

The first I knew of the military coup was being awakened by the noise of rifles. My first thought was that the Korean war had suddenly become hot and that firing was taking place on the thirty-eighth parallel. Within twenty minutes I heard that it was our own military coup. Like myself, everyone began to feel safe and secure, welcoming the new situation not because we believed in a military coup but because we knew that was the last resort to fall back upon. The military forces had had consistent training of their personnel, particularly of the officers' group, ever since the war and had a better prepared leadership potential than any other, as a group, in the country. Over the radio General Doyoung Chang, Chief of Staff, was broadcasting the change, and we all felt that the country was on the right track once again.

We were disillusioned with politicians and political parties. Many of the politicians were our friends and we thought they were all right at heart, wanting to do the best for the country; but once they got the political machinery into their own hands, they found temptation too great and either became self-seeking officials or turned into absolutely impotent, helpless, and useless individuals. Something was wrong with the system or with the group who operated the system, as well as with the general populace which had had no training in the traditions and responsibilities of democratic government.

As we listened to the radio announcing the fact that both the Upper and Lower Houses were dissolved, we applauded with a sigh of relief. Away with the Senate and the Assembly which only ate up the national treasury and created confusion, complications, and chaos within the nation! Our feeling of relief was not a reaction against running the nation by elected representatives within a constitutional government. But for some reason these representatives either could not or would not function properly. Something was wrong somewhere. We must stop to re-think and re-start our national course of democracy along lines more realistically adapted to our situation at the present stage of development. To what better group of leaders could we entrust this task than to the leadership of the military forces which had already seen the need and started to supply it? People in increasing numbers began to support and cooperate with the new leadership.

In the middle of June some concern was felt over the fact that friendly nations and peoples abroad found it difficult to understand and feel about our new military leadership as we did from within. At the suggestion and with the support of responsible groups both in the government and among the people, Dr. Kyung-jik Hahn of Young-Nak church, Mr. Doo-sun Choi of *Dong-A* daily newspaper, and I were sent on a goodwill mission to the United States. It was on the whole a very successful one.

We went straight to Washington and spent four days explaining our new situation in Korea to friends in government circles and the press, and to religious and social organizations. We had also very helpful times with Korean residents in and around Washington. Then we went to New York City and met with many groups. The urgency of some other errands made it necessary for me to return to Korea immediately from New York. But the other two members, Dr. Hahn and Mr. Choi, continued the tour, stopping over in Boston, Chicago, San Francisco, Los Angeles, Honolulu, and in Tokyo.

Just as I was starting out from New York for Seoul, the news came that there had been a shift in the leadership of the military junta. General Do-young Chang was replaced by General Chung-hi Park as the Chairman of the Supreme Council. I knew they were good friends and had worked together for many years with mutual trust and confidence. Therefore, one would be just as good as the other. But I knew General Chang personally much better and could answer all the questions asked about him. So upon return I went straight to General Park and learned directly the answers to questions about him through a heart-to-heart talk. From then on I could and would support him without reservation.

Some friends have asked me, "How is it that you are sent on government errands by the leaders of all the different regimes?" This question seems to imply that I am either fickle or lacking in fidelity. Except for the one regime which misunderstood me as aligned to a particular political party, from Dr. Rhee to General Park I have been asked to serve the country on temporary errands from time to time. All I have tried to do is to be ready to serve the cause of my country as I believe all good citizens should whenever there is a need.

I do not serve a particular individual, much less a political party. I am always for my country and therefore, not for any political reasons but from patriotic motives, can cooperate with the individual or the party that bears the responsibility of the nation. In this way I am able to serve my nation consistently in spite of the changes in leaders—in peaceful times as well as in revolutions.

XIII

MILESTONES

This is a personal story, but my life has been lived against a backdrop of turbulent events and inevitably these events are a part of my story. But there were intervals of quiet when the normal interests of life could be observed.

Two important milestones in my life were reached during the period of relative calm after the shattering events of the Korean War and its bewildering armistice, and while indications of the 1960 political conflict were as yet an indistinct cloud on the horizon.

The year 1958 marked my fortieth year of teaching and administration at Ewha, and my colleagues and friends made it an occasion for congratulation and recognition.

In spite of my protests, a statue of me was erected on the campus. An honor I especially appreciated was the publication of two books. One was a compilation of articles on women's development and their contribution to Korean culture. The articles, written mostly by our own leading women, dealt with women in Korean literature, in art, in education and other professions, in the home, and in national and social life.

A special celebration took place on May 9. A recognition service was held in our Welch-Ryang Auditorium and later in the day our new library building was dedicated and named in my honor. Many gifts were received from personal friends and from friends of the University. The most touching one was a horizontal, framed picture entitled "Heavenly Peaches," painted by one of our eminent contemporary artists, Mr. Ki-Chang Kim. This was a present from a group of girls' high school principals who had been my close friends for a long time. Among them were Mr. Dong-sik Cho, Miss Sook Chong Lee, and Mrs. Sin-duk Whang. The painting symbolized their wish that I feed upon the "heavenly peaches" and live a long and healthy life. It hangs in New House where we gather together from time to time for fellowship.

In less than a year, on February 27, 1959, my sixtieth birthday arrived. According to Korean tradition there are three most important dates in one's life: the wedding day, the *whan-kap* (sixtieth birthday), and the day one passes away into the unknown. It is customary that one's children gather together for the celebration of the *whan-kap* of their parents, planning for it, paying for all the expenses, and acting as hosts and hostesses.

As the first important date had never arrived for me, which meant I had no children to celebrate my second important date, my colleagues at the University began to think in terms of making it an institutional event. To this I gave an absolute veto. "No matter how important the date is to me, it is a private matter. I do not believe in mixing private and public affairs in such a manner. I will have a grand celebration and feast ready, all in proper traditional forms. You are invited to enjoy the day with me as my personal friends and not as professional colleagues."

However, eight of my friends made plans and took the entire responsibility for the event as though they were my children. After that I called them my children, although several of them were near my own age. They were Miss Unsook Saw, Mrs. Maria Pak Lee, Miss Sook Chong Lee, Mrs. Hyun-Sil Kim Lee, Mrs. Youngyi Kim

Sihn, Miss Ki-Hong Cho, Miss Okgill Kim, and Mr. Dongill Arthur Kim.

The significance attributed to *whan-kap*, or the six-tieth birthday, lies in the fact that in our old tradition it marks the end of a life cycle and the beginning of another. The old oriental way of counting the years was by combination of ten positive and twelve negative forces. They make up sixty years, which are considered one cycle. When one is finished, the second cycle of the same combinations begins over again. In the older days when the life span was short, not many people lived to finish one and begin the other. It was a rare enough event to be greatly celebrated. When longevity was wished for friends, one used to say, "I hope you will live to have a grand *whan-kap* celebration." In Korea this custom still is respected and we celebrate *whan-kap*, although we feel quite young at sixty.

Perhaps the best way of describing my party is to quote the account which Mrs. Yun-sook Yoo Lee, my secretary, wrote for the benefit of those who were not present.

On a sunny and beautiful spring day, February 27, 1959, there was a happy occasion at Tong-il-kak in Dr. Kim's downtown house. The occasion was Dr. Helen Kim's *whan-kap chan chi,* the 60th birthday. Starting with the first two guests at 8:30 in the morning, several hundred people gathered by noon, and the house was full of people, men and women, old and young, dressed in their best. They all looked gay and happy and even excited. As if to take part in blessing the occasion, birds in the pine trees were singing under the clear blue sky.

The *whan-kap* table, a special feature of the day, which took several days to prepare by the specialists, old and skilled in this work, was in the center of the room ready for Dr. Kim. It was wonderful to see. The table was very big and high and beautiful. Apples, pears, grapefruit, dates, chestnuts, pine nuts, walnuts, and various kinds of Korean cakes and cookies were piled up in columns two feet high. Ewha girls helped to pile up the pine nuts by putting them on to pine needles in bunches of five. Scrolls and screens of oriental paintings behind the table made a setting for Dr. Kim.

At noon Dr. Kim appeared in her *whan-kap* dress and crown before the guests, who were all surprised and happy to see her queenlike appearance. The *whan-kap* dress, which was designed and made by Ewha Home Economics Department professors, was white silk. The long train and belt with hand embroidered symbols of pear flowers added beauty and grace. A most gracious and happy queen sat down before the table.

Immediately following Dr. Kim's appearance, the ceremony was started with a thanksgiving service led by Mrs. Maria Pak Lee, Vice-President of Ewha. Mrs. Grace P. Chang, an Ewha graduate and principal of Kyunggi Girls' High School, offered the opening prayer. Miss Yun-sook Moh read her own poem written for Dr. Kim, and Mrs. Cha Kyung Kim Sim, who set it to music, sang it most beautifully. The 23rd Psalm was read, and the hymn "To Higher Ground" was sung; the Lord's Prayer was offered in unison.

The program then turned to stately bows to the day's queen. This bowing is an expression of high respect and hearty congratulation for the sixty years of happy and fruitful life she has lived, and sincere wishes for the coming years. Dr. Kim's relatives, who were formally dressed in *dang-e*, were the first group to bow. *Dang-e* is the half formal robe in green silk worn over the colorful long skirt and the *cho-gori*. And the bowing goes clear down with hands and heads touching the floor. This was followed by the bowing of the guests. They bowed in couples, in family groups, in groups of children and adults. A group of cute boys and girls from Ewha Kindergarten, several girls and boys from Ewha Demonstration Middle and High Schools, and six students representing six colleges from Ewha University, also bowed. Everybody was smiling, and happiness and joy overflowed the house.

At about one o'clock, according to Korean custom, *kooksoo* (noodles), which symbolizes happy and long life, was served to Dr. Kim and to the guests. With so many guests, the house was crowded beyond capacity, but the cheerful guests knew no discomfort because of the spirit of merriment. All through the day and the one following visitors were served delicacies like those on the *whan-kap* table. Later this was dismantled and the delicacies were distributed to neighbors and friends.

An interesting and amusing program took place after the lunch, and the whole day passed very quickly with singing and special dances performed by children from the Ewha kindergarten. As is the Korean custom at *whan-kap*, old Korean musicians in red formal dress and in black hats played the accompaniment for the singers and dancers. The old instruments that they played looked odd, but the principles of wind, string, brass, etc. were the same as for more modern instruments.

Many birthday gifts were received from near and far and piled up in one corner of the room. Among them was a big scroll of caligraphy on which was a poem about Dr. Kim, composed and written by President Syngman Rhee. A large crayon drawing by the children of Ewha Primary was also a great delight to Dr. Kim. After opening the gift parcels, Dr. Kim said that as a way of expressing her deep gratitude for these expressions of love by her friends, she plans to build with the money gifts a memorial church and to establish a scholarship fund for Ewha students. Once again her friends were deeply touched and moved by her response, which proved to be another act of thinking of and giving herself to others.

The following day was also spent in joy with many visitors. In two days, several hundred friends visited Dr. Kim. She must have been surprised to see so many. Two friends came as far as from New Milford, Connecticut. They were Misses Josephine Brown and Mildred Owen. Numerous congratulatory cards, letters, and cables were received from far and wide. The *whan-kap chan chi* was a splendid occasion, revealing to Dr. Kim some fruits of her sixty years of strenuous efforts.

Such pomp and gaiety, dignity and grandeur at the celebration of my *whan-kap* meant I had attained a certain age.

When the end of the academic year arrived in March of the same year, I felt definitely that the time had come for me to retire. I felt that I was led to do some Christian evangelistic work, not in any formal way but just by being and doing good among people—loving them as I have never loved before. I tendered my resignation as the president of Ewha to the Board of Trustees. But the Board thought differently and laid my resignation on the table. My retirement had to be postponed for the time being. And our university continued to grow, with more students and more buildings to care for them.

Early in 1960 our Ewha Legal Holding Body completed the new International Night College building. The International Night College had been under The Korean Methodist Church, serving the ambitious young people who had to work in the daytime but who wanted an opportunity for higher education. It was meeting a great need, but lacked financial support. The Korean Methodist Church could not provide this, and Bishop Lew felt that another sponsor must be found. In order to keep the Night College within the Methodist fold, he had challenged our corporation to take and run it. As loyal Methodists, we answered the challenge and began to rebuild the Night College. Fortunately we found a leader, Professor Hyung Kyu Woo of the English Department, who was able to handle the difficult situation. Somehow the much needed building was finished and that fact alone boosted the morale of the teachers and student body of the Night College to the extent that they were able to make a new start.

Because this building was in use only during the evening hours, we felt that day classes could be started for people who worked at night. The new Ministry of Education had a strong policy of not increasing the college population in the whole country since it was generally considered that the number of our college graduates far exceeded the job opportunities available for them. The authorities attempted to curb this natural tendency by limiting the enrollment of all colleges and universities. So instead of giving us permission for college work, we were requested to open and run a girls' high school during the day. There was an acute emergency in the shortage of high schools to accommodate the increasing number of boys and girls ready to enter. Our corporation decided to help meet this need since the building stood empty during the day. Again under the leadership of Professor Hyung Kyu Woo, Kum-Nan High School was started in April 1960, and is fast becoming one of the standard girls' high schools in Seoul.

Ewha's seventy-fifth Founder's Day anniversary was observed in May, 1961. For months everyone concerned had been making plans and preparations for a big celebration. The military coup, which presented a totally new situation with a strong austerity program, had made it seem at first impossible to go ahead with the celebration. But with careful modification and under the generous permission of the authorities we were able to carry out all our original plans.

As was usual on Founder's Day, in the morning a great convocation took place in the stadium. Among our special guests were Dr. E. Thillayampalam and Miss Mary Abraham who had come to be with us from Isa-

bella Thoburn College of Lucknow, India. Isabella Thoburn and Ewha were started in the same year by the same
Woman's Foreign Missionary Society of the Methodist Episcopal Church of the United States. So we had
planned to have exchange visits of the presidents at the
anniversary celebrations and an exchange of professors
for one year. According to this plan I already had been
at Isabella Thoburn College during the third week of
its celebration in February. And in return, Dr. Thillayampalam, the Principal, came to be with us during our
anniversary week. With her came Miss Mary Abraham,
who stayed through the next academic year and taught
Indian History and English. In exchange, Mrs. Chung-
soon Sung Kim, of our Physical Education Department,
taught that year at Isabella Thoburn College.

Following the anniversary convocation, we had the
crowning of the May Queen and other colorful drills
and exercises during the day. Numerous plays, exhibits,
concerts, and gatherings of alumnae filled the rest of
the week. Several publications, both by the faculty and
students, were brought out in celebration of this event;
and a large classroom building was under construction
to commemorate this great occasion. Recently, seventy-
five thousand dollars came from a legacy of the Woman's
Foreign Missionary Society, the founder of Ewha, to be
applied to the cost of this building, which is not yet
completed.

During the second week in October we held the
seventy-fifth anniversary revival meeting with the help
of an evangelistic mission led by Dr. Harry Denman and
Dr. J. Manning Potts. We had great success in nearing
our goal of helping every individual who walks the
campus of Ewha find its real Founder, the Creator of the
universe and the Lover of men.

Under the auspices of Ewha University and the Christian Teachers Association, the mission involved not only Ewha but more than a dozen high schools. In addition to Dr. Denman and Dr. Potts, the members of the team were Mrs. C. Lloyd Daugherty, the Reverend G. Eugene Durham, Mr. and Mrs. R. H. Smith, Dr. Walter K. Kerr, Dr. and Mrs. Charles W. Grant, Mr. A. S. Mertz, Dr. Leonard D. Peale, the Reverend Lloyd A. Gustafson, and the Reverend Howard W. Ellis.

Nearly thirty thousand students were reached in the mission. Over eight thousand made Christian decisions and a total of more than sixteen hundred were baptized.

Many baptisms took place later in the high schools, mostly at commencement time. The chief baptismal service took place at Ewha University on Sunday morning. In this one service, one thousand two hundred eighty-nine students, faculty members, and employees of the University were baptized. Fourteen ministers participated in the service, including Bishop Hazen G. Werner and Bishop Chong Pil Kim. It was a glorious service and one long to be remembered by those who participated in it.

During the preceding two years the faculty and student body of Ewha had been praying and working on plans to have three representatives sent to Pakistan to share with the girls of that land the blessings of life we have received through Christian education. Bishop Chandu Ray of the Anglican Church in Pakistan needed trained Christian teachers for the schools under his jurisdiction. Three Ewha graduates, Eun-ja Kim, Chae-ok Chun, and Sung-ja Cho, volunteered for this service; and our students and faculty assumed their support as missionary teachers. For over a year their visas had been held up and the outlook was very discouraging. At last the visas came through and on October 31 all three of them—Eun-ja, Chae-ok, and Sung-ja—flew away on wings to fulfill their mission in Pakistan.

They are working in Anglican girls' high schools under the guidance of Bishop Chandu Ray. Since they have been working in Pakistan, all of them have acquired the Urdu language, so they are using both Urdu and English as media of instruction. They have identified themselves with the people there and have won the love and appreciation of their colleagues.

So successful has been their work that Bishop Chandu Ray asked for three more girls for three additional institutions. We did not see how we could finance these extra teachers. However, the three institutions were encouraged to take the responsibility for their support and the East Asia Christian Conference agreed to pay their travel expenses. And so as soon as we get three girls ready, they will accompany Eun-ja Kim, Chae-ok Chun, and Sung-ja Cho when they return to Pakistan from their furloughs.

This indeed was the crowning finale of Ewha's seventy-fifth anniversary celebration, symbolic and prophetic of Ewha's next seventy-five years of service, not only to Korea but to the world.

There are other graduates whose work and life indicate certain trends for the fulfillment of Ewha's goals. One is Hei-sook Lee. She had been one of the leaders in our student movement to visit villages and carry on an enlightenment program during their summer and winter holidays. Hei-sook is the first graduate who took this as her lifework. She saw a need that she could help fill and she grew in love for the village people so much that she went back to live with and to serve them. Her teachers are helping her with some funds and materials;

otherwise, she is on her own. Nobody has employed and sent her, so she has no place to look for regular support. "Freely ye have received, freely give" is the command she is obeying.

Another is Dr. Hun-Kyung Ban, a graduate of our Medical College. Ever since her graduation she has been working in our practice hospital. She has been giving all her spare time to ministering to the poor people who cannot afford hospitalization. This work carries her into remote villages as well as to institutions for the poor and homeless. She receives some financial help from her teachers and friends to pay for the medicines she must have. She bears all other expenses, besides giving her time. She has restored sight to many who had lost it, largely due to mistreatment or lack of care. In one village a man came to her thinking he was going blind. Upon examination she found a growth over his eye and skillfully removed it. It was a seed of corn beginning to sprout in his eye! Village people call her "heaven-sent angel" as she moves and ministers among them under the spell of constant inspiration from the Great Physician, the Master whom she serves. One can understand the *raison d'etre* of Ewha Medical College as graduates like Dr. Ban minister to the poor and the sick.

In August, I went to New Haven, Connecticut, to attend the meetings of the Theological Education Fund Committee of the International Missionary Council. The work of this committee is to administer a special fund of four million dollars—two million given by John D. Rockefeller, Jr., through the Sealantic Fund, and two million matched by the different Boards of Missions. The purpose of the fund is to upgrade, improve, and strengthen theological education in younger church areas. On my return trip I had scheduled a few stopovers with friends whom I never seemed to find time to visit.

I was already in the Cleveland area when I received a cable calling me back to Korea immediately. The cable did not indicate why I had to be summoned, but I knew I must return at once. I was then having a happy reunion with some former Ewha teachers—Mrs. Mertie I. Grau of Kent, Ohio, and Misses Jeannette and Esther Hulbert and Miss Myrta Stover of Cleveland. Miss Jeannette Hulbert had been my teacher during my student days at Ewha College. All these visits had to be cut off abruptly, and two more were cancelled. Thanks to American efficiency in the communication and transportation services and to the timely help of friends at each point on the way, I was back in Seoul on Friday, the eighth of September—twenty-four hours after leaving Cleveland. This included the layover of nine and one-half hours in Tokyo.

On arrival I felt relieved to find that there was nothing more serious than the need of my prompt attention to a new government decree affecting my resignation from the presidency of Ewha. The age for the retirement of all workers in schools and universities had been set by the Military Government at sixty. I told Ewha Board members that God was using the Military Government to do what they had refused to do two years before. Willingly and gladly I went about the business which had to be finished by the end of the month. Students and faculty members and friends everywhere acted as though my funeral were in progress.

My colleagues gave me wonderful cooperation in the selection and initiation of my successor. Our problem was not that of having no candidates, but of selection among several ready for the job. After consultations among individuals and groups, a unanimous conclusion was happily reached. Miss Okgill Kim, a graduate of Ewha, who had already served the University for seventeen years in all the different roles of teacher and administrative assistant, was nominated to the Board. The Board elected her unanimously to the presidency of Ewha Womans University. After this news was known, graduates and friends, students and parents complimented and congratulated us upon our selection. This great unanimity forecasts confidence in the future of Ewha.

The day for my retirement and for the inauguration of the new president was September 30, 1961. This was my last chance to honor some of my colleagues who had worked side by side with me for the last two decades and had made notable contributions to the development of the University. Prior to the inauguration I took the liberty of conferring honorary degrees upon the new president, Okgill Kim, upon Dean Yong-Koo Pang and Professors Shinsil Kim and Mary Lee, and upon Dr. Burnice Jarman, who had directed our Self-Study Survey during the year. Following this I had the great privilege of handing over the sacred responsibility for the care and growth of the University, with all its students and faculty, to Dr. Okgill Kim. With courage and devotion she accepted it most graciously. At the very end of the service, the Board of Trustees honored me by naming me President Emeritus.

As Chairman of the Legal Holding Body I am still able to help Ewha and the new President. In this capacity I also have an overall responsibility for International Night College and Kum-Nan Girls' High School.

Leaving Wichita House, the President's residence on

campus, was no problem, because a house to retire to had already been under construction near the campus since spring and was just being finished. Who has built it and how? We just say that God had been getting it ready in time for my use while nobody even dreamed that it would be needed in September. The fund for it had been started by Miss Florence Gibson as early as 1945 when she knew that my house had to be sold during the war. She left some money in her will for that purpose. The fund kept growing from the acquisition of Victory House in Pusan and the sale of Town House in Seoul. A Korean friend had helped to clear the debt on Town House, thus making a considerable contribution to the cost of the new house. The banks were very cooperative, so at last it could be built. Through the friends of Ewha, God has built and paid for this house which we now call "New House." It was ready for me to retire to, a house with all the conveniences, comfort, and beauty that I need, and more.

As for the future—I know it will be full and rewarding, come what may. After my *whan-kap* and then retirement from the Ewha presidency, my age seemed to be one of the chief topics of conversation among my friends. I am glad they think me young looking but I hope I am young thinking and acting too. After all, my heritage would point to my having a number more years on this earth. My father lived seventy-nine years with poor health and without the help of modern medicine. My mother lived ninety years; she might still be living if she had not been subjected to the shock and privations of the Korean War.

The more I think about it, the more I believe a sane and healthy old age would be a desirable thing. If God so permits, I will welcome it and have a wonderful time with it. Life with leisure could be creative. There would be enough time for all the things that I have wanted to do but which have had to be postponed. At least there will be more time for greater attempts at creative activities since I am no longer carrying burdens of administration as I have done for so many years.

All my life I have gone forward in faith—faith in my family, my friends, my college, my country, and in God's providence. In retrospect many things seem like miracles —my education at a time when it was only important for girls to be married, and yet the way was cleared for me to have my PhD when I was thirty-two, the first Korean woman recipient. When I began my presidency at Ewha College there were about six hundred students and but eight buildings. At my retirement Ewha had become a university with seven colleges and an enrollment of over eight thousand, and with more than twenty-five buildings. Faith and hard work have made this possible.

I do not think I can state the principle of my faith as such. I studied courses in Religion during my college days and I have read and studied Christian literature all my life, but when one is busy living his life from day to day, religion becomes an experience rather than a creed.

The guiding principle of my life has been, in one word, Christ. What Christ means to us—what He has done and why He has done it and how He has done it— all this put together forms the historical basis of Christian experience. So when issues have come up for decisions, Christ has been the guiding word or the guiding principle. When the one word, Christ, enters my consciousness, then it is easy to think and to judge what would be right or wrong for me to do. What would

Christ have done? What would He want me to do under these circumstances?

And then I would mention a second characteristic of my faith which cannot be called a principle, but rather a practice—taking the problem or the issue to God in prayer and waiting for His guidance. The answer has come each time, not as a mystical experience but as a thoroughly practical one. Into my mind the light would come, with conviction that it was a definite guidance from God in answer to my prayer; and I would follow this guidance without hesitation. I remember a student telling me about her thoughts at a chapel service when she heard me pray God to give us our much needed library. She questioned in her mind, "Our President cannot be that naive, and yet she cannot be insincere in her prayers." Very soon she saw the library building going up, and then she said she understood for the first time the connection between prayers and the realization of the objects we pray for.

In faith when I was a youth I accepted special responsibility for our womanhood. In faith I have served all my life in whatever way I could to bring freedom and enlightenment to our people. My faith has been justified. In my lifelong experience of God's grace I have always found it to be just enough—in other words, sufficient. God has never been extravagant, or stingy, in His constant bestowal of grace.

APPENDIX

Recognition on a national and international scale has been accorded Helen Kim for her remarkable religious, educational, civic, and cultural contribution to her country and to the world. Honorary doctoral degrees have been conferred upon her by Ohio Wesleyan, Boston, Cornell, and Centro Escalor universities. In 1963 she was the recipient of three distinguished citations: Certificate of Order of Cultural Merit of the Republic of Korea, the Ramon Magsaysay Award for Public Service, and The Upper Room Citation for Leadership in World Christian Fellowship. These citations are reproduced on the following pages.

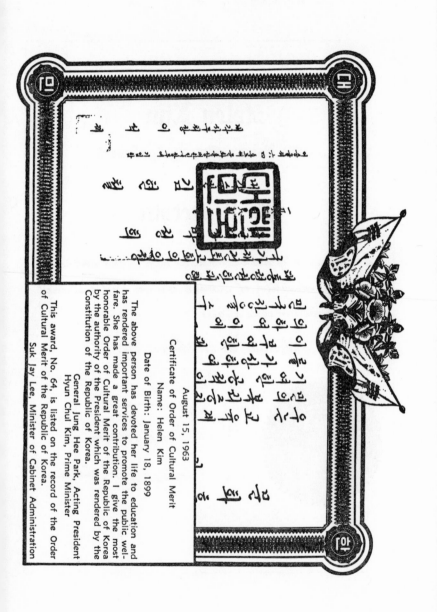

August 15, 1963

Certificate of Order of Cultural Merit

Name: Helen Kim

Date of Birth: January 18, 1899

The above person has devoted her life to education and has rendered important services to promote the public welfare. She has made a great contribution. I give the most honorable Order of Cultural Merit of the Republic of Korea by the authority of the President which was rendered by the Constitution of the Republic of Korea.

General Jung Hee Park, Acting President
Hyun Chul Kim, Prime Minister

This award, No. 64, is listed on the record of the Order of Cultural Merit of the Republic of Korea.

Suk Jay Lee, Minister of Cabinet Administration

Helen Kim

1963 Ramon Magsaysay Award

for

Public Service

in recognition of her indomitable role in the emancipation and education of Korean women and sustained participation in civic affairs.

Manila on 31 August 1963

Belen H. Abreu

The Upper Room

Citation for 1963

Helen Kim

THE PERSON SELECTED TO RECEIVE THE UPPER ROOM CITATION IN 1963 FOR
LEADERSHIP IN WORLD CHRISTIAN FELLOWSHIP

Christian educator, scholar, administrator, teacher at Ewha Woman's College, 1918-1939; president, 1939-1945; president of Ewha Woman's University, 1945-1961; world Christian leader; official representative of the Republic of Korea, both at home and abroad; founder and director of national and world woman's organizations.

Chairman of the Board of Trustees of National YWCA of Korea; director of the Office of Public Information of ROK; Publisher of *Korea Times*; president of Korean Association of University Women; member of the Executive Committee of the National UNESCO; vice-president of the International Missionary Council; vice-chairman of the Higher Education Advisory Committee; member of the Board of Methodist Theological Seminary, Seoul; vice-president of the Korean Red Cross; member of the Board of the Korean Anti-Communist League; president of the Korean Christian Teachers Association.

Member of international conferences: Student Christian Federation Conference, Peking, China, 1922; Conference of Far East Christian Leaders, Shanghai, China, 1928; International Missionary Council, Jerusalem, 1928; General Conference of the Methodist Episcopal Church, 1928 and 1932; World Council of YWCA, Hangchow, China, 1946; Korean Mission to the United Nations, Paris, 1949, New York, 1956, 1957, 1958, 1959; Joint Committee of International Missionary Council and World Council of Churches, Oxford, England, 1955; Herrenalb, West Germany, 1956; New Haven, Connecticut, 1957; Spittal, Austria, 1959; World Congress of the International Federation of University Women, Paris, 1956; The 14th World Convention of Christian Education, Tokyo, Japan, 1958; International Committee of Red Cross, Geneva, 1959; International Missionary Council, Paris, 1959; International Federation of University Women, Helsinki, 1959; Tenth World Methodist Conference, Oslo, Norway, 1961; Theological Education Fund Committee, IMC, New Haven, Connecticut, 1961; Arnoldshain, Taunus, Germany, 1962; World Council of Churches, New Delhi, India, 1961; XII UNESCO Conference, Paris, 1962; Asian Peoples' Anti-Communist League, Tokyo, Japan, 1962; Magsaysay Award for Public Service, Philippines, 1963; Order of Cultural Merit, Republic of Korea, 1963.

HELEN KIM

A lifetime dedicated to Christian education of Korean women, a world figure who has not lost the common touch, a crusader for human rights, a devoted servant of Christ and the church universal, committed to world brotherhood, world Christian fellowship, and the kingdom of God.

Presented at the Citation Dinner, National Press Club, Washington, D. C.

October 1, 1963

THE UPPER ROOM, NASHVILLE, TENNESSEE

Editor